HIKING OHIO

Scenic Trails
of the Buckeye State

by Robert Folzenlogen

WILLOW PRESS
Glendale, Ohio

ISBN: 0-9620685-2-7
Library of Congress Catalog Card Number: 90-70629

Published by Willow Press, Glendale, Ohio
Printed by Otto Zimmerman & Son Company, Inc.,
  Newport, Kentucky
Typesetting by Debbie Metz, Mass Marketing, Inc.,
  Cincinnati, Ohio

Photos by author
Maps by author, adapted from those provided by O.D.N.R.,
  County Park Districts and other areas covered in this guide.
Cover artwork by Jan Jolley

For Darcy, Sarah,
Zach and Ally

ACKNOWLEDGEMENTS

My sincere thanks to the many Forest Rangers, Park Managers and Organization Secretaries who provided background information for this book. The following individuals and groups deserve special mention for their contributions to my research:

The Buckeye Trail Association
R. Conder, Chief Ranger, Salt Fork State Park
Jon Dobney, Park Manager, Caesar Creek State Park
Mary Hess, Coordinator, Ohio Chapter, Rails-to-Trails
    Conservancy
James Little, Park Naturalist, Mohican-Memorial State Park
The Nature Conservancy, Ohio Chapter
Ohio Department of Natural Resources
Christopher Schillizzi, Interpretive Specialist, Cuyahoga
    Valley National Recreation Area
George Sholtis, Ranger, Lake Loramie State Park
Greg Smith, Assistant Forest Manager, Mohican-Memorial
    State Forest
Sandy Spayd, Kelleys Island Chamber of Commerce

Thanks also to Debbie Metz, at Mass Marketing, Inc., and Jan Jolley, at Otto Zimmerman & Son Company, Inc., for their creative and technical assistance.

Finally, my thanks to Darcy, Sarah, Zach and Ally for their company and inspiration. Darcy's editorial work and her advice regarding the design and content of this guide were essential to its production.

CONTENTS

FOREWORD

Those of us who love to hike are always looking for new and interesting areas to explore. This guide offers over 100 day hikes, spread across Ohio, chosen with the goal of exposing the reader to the diverse topography, geology, flora and fauna that characterize our State. The areas included in this guide are, for the most part, free and open to the public throughout the year. A few of the preserves charge a nominal parking or day-usage fee. Areas that require special permission for entrance and private recreation lands that charge significant entry fees are not included.

Emphasis is placed on reasonable day hikes, in the 2-12 mile range, permitting sufficient time for rest, exploration and nourishment along the way. Those interested in longer, multi-day backpack trips are referred to other guides, such as **Backpack Loops in Southern Ohio**, by Robert H. Ruchhoft, listed in the Bibliography.

Each of the hikes covered in this book is accompanied by a map which illustrates the trail route, water drainages, parking areas, trailhead location and points of interest along the way. Narratives describe the route and provide information regarding the historical background, natural features, local flora and resident fauna of the area. Directions to each area are also included.

Throughout this guide, frequent reference is made to geologic history. Rock strata, glacial remnants, fossil beds and vegetation patterns all reflect the natural evolution of Ohio. Appendix I thus provides a synopsis of geologic time, with emphasis on regional phenomena. Knowledge of these past events will add to your enjoyment of nature's present-day handiwork.

Appendix II lists organizations in Ohio that are devoted to the protection of our natural resources. Indeed, most of the areas covered in this guide owe their continued existence to these conservation-minded groups. Your support of their efforts will ensure the future preservation of our dwindling open spaces and critical wildlife habitat.

When to Go

Hiking is a year-round activity. While the beginner often shuns a cold weather jaunt, experienced hikers know that the invigorating days of October through April offer the best hiking of the year. Pesky insects are gone, vistas are broader and the dry, frozen ground offers better footing. For those averse to snakes, winter is a good time to avoid our three poisonous species, the timber rattler and copperhead of the Appalachian Plateau and the massasauga of northern Ohio marshlands.

In reality, each season holds its special delights for the hiker. Autumn colors emblazen the woodlands during the crisp month of October. Forest wildflowers are most abundant in April, before the burgeoning canopy closes out the sun. Prairie flowers peak in late summer as golds and purples explode across the grasslands. In spring and fall, birdwatchers head for the wetlands to catch the tide of migrant waterfowl and shorebirds. Native mammals are generally most conspicuous during the barren months of winter and the quiet, snowladen forest is a sure cure for cabin fever.

Some of the more popular hiking areas are especially crowded on warm weather weekends and weekday hiking is recommended if possible. Resident birds and mammals tend to be most active, and thus most visible, during the early morning and late daylight hours. Some creatures, such as white-tailed deer, mink, raccoons, opossums, flying squirrels and most owls, are best found at dusk.

What to Bring

First and foremost, a hiking companion is strongly recommended. While a solitary stroll in the forest is surely a peaceful escape, an unexpected fall or injury can be disastrous for the loner, especially in winter.

Water and nourishment should be carried on longer hikes. Natural sources of water, no matter how clear and inviting, should not be consumed. A compass is often helpful and binoculars will add to the enjoyment of wildlife and vistas. Field guides illustrating the native flora and fauna of Ohio are also indispensable for the amateur naturalist.

For the serious hiker, especially those of us with unstable ankles, a good pair of waterproof hiking boots is a year-round necessity. Among the seasonal requirements, insect repellant is mandatory during the warmer months.

Low Impact Hiking

The conservationist's motto regarding the use of wild places is to *"Take only photos and leave only footprints."* Be sure to pack out any trash that you bring into the preserves. Wildflowers, plants and native creatures should be left undisturbed. Collection of nuts and berries is permitted in some areas but leaving them for the local wildlife makes good ecological sense.

Your attention to the protection and preservation of these natural areas will ensure their continued health and vitality. Finally, after enjoying these oases of life, lend your support to the conservation effort by contributing time and/or money to the organizations listed in Appendix II of this book. Without the continued vigilance of these groups, what little remains of Ohio's natural heritage would soon be lost.

— Robert Folzenlogen

KEY TO MAPS

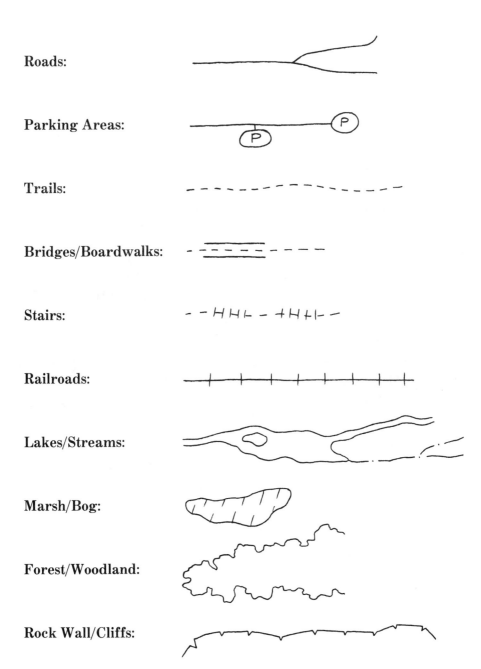

Roads:

Parking Areas:

Trails:

Bridges/Boardwalks:

Stairs:

Railroads:

Lakes/Streams:

Marsh/Bog:

Forest/Woodland:

Rock Wall/Cliffs:

LOCATION OF HIKING AREAS

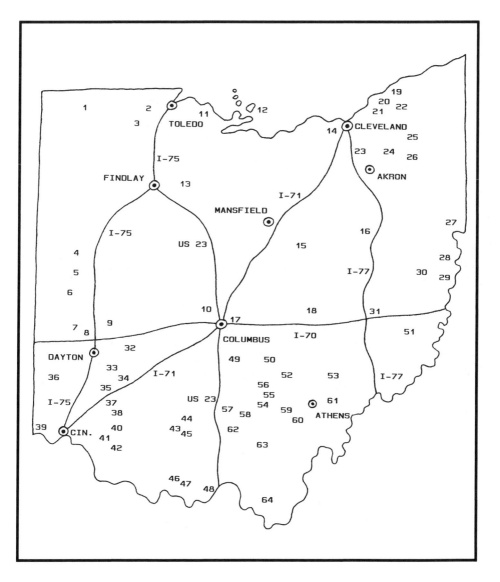

HIKING AREAS IN THIS GUIDE

I. THE BUCKEYE TRAIL

Founded in 1959, the Buckeye Trail Association is a nonprofit corporation dedicated to the maintenance of the **Buckeye Trail**. This Trail, now over 1200 miles in length, is the longest hiking trail in Ohio and the longest continuous trail in any State. Its route utilizes city streets, country roads, forest paths and abandoned roadbeds. A large portion of the Trail coincides with the route of the **North Country Trail**, which stretches from New York to North Dakota.

The **Buckeye Trail** loops through Ohio, connecting the varied geophysical regions of our State. In northeastern Ohio it winds past glacial lakes, bogs and stands of hemlock. In southeastern Ohio it negotiates the forested hills, cool streams and rock-walled gorges of the Appalachian Plateau. Heading west, the Trail enters the fertile farmlands of Ohio's till plains and snakes past several of our larger reservoirs. Angling northward, the **Buckeye Trail** follows the abandoned towpath of the Miami-Erie Canal and then turns eastward, crossing through the Lake Plains of northern Ohio.

The Trail's primary route is blazed with blue while side trails are marked with white slashes. Mileage signs are spaced along the route, noting distance in both miles and kilometers.

A complete discussion of the **Buckeye Trail** and its route is beyond the scope of this guide. However, portions of the Trail will be noted within many of the hiking areas and its route is labeled with **BT** throughout the book. The map on page 7 depicts the general course of the **Buckeye Trail** through Ohio and the numbers correspond to the areas in this guide where the Trail can be accessed.

The Buckeye Trail Association provides detailed maps for 25 sections of the Trail and also publishes a guide to 18 short day hikes along the **Buckeye Trail** (see Bibliography). Membership in the Buckeye Trail Association is currently $10/individual or $10/family. For information regarding membership, maps, publications, organized hikes and volunteer activities, contact the Association at P.O. Box 254, Worthington, Ohio, 43085. Your financial and/or active support will ensure the future protection and maintenance of this historic and natural corridor.

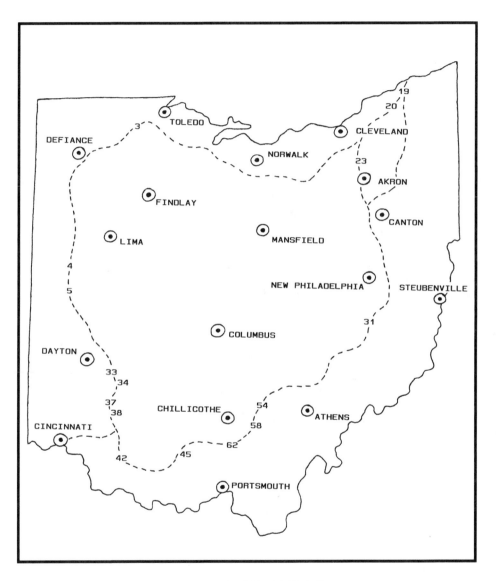

THE BUCKEYE TRAIL

Numbers correspond to Hiking Areas in this guide where the Trail can be accessed.

II. HIKING AREAS OF NORTHWEST OHIO

1. Goll Woods

2. Oak Openings Preserve

3. Maumee River Parks

4. Miami-Erie Trail

5. Lake Loramie State Park

6. Stillwater Prairie Preserve

7. Englewood Reserve

8. Aullwood Audubon Center

9. Charleston Falls Preserve

10. Highbanks Metro Park

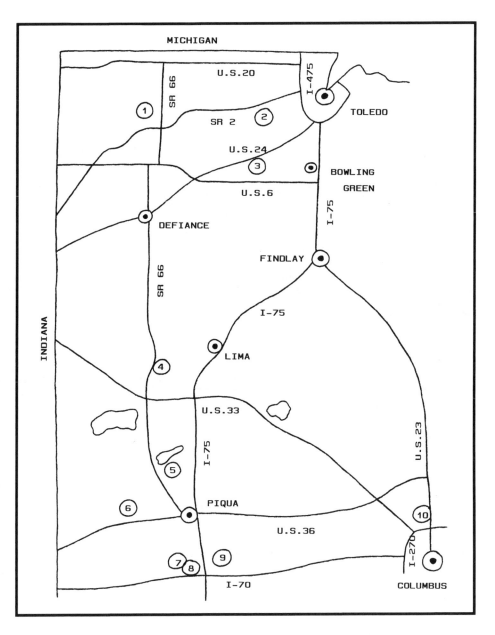

HIKING AREAS OF NORTHWEST OHIO

9

1   GOLL WOODS STATE NATURE PRESERVE

Distance: 3.75 miles
Terrain: flat to gently rolling

Goll Woods, an 80 acre oasis of forest in the flat farmlands of northwest Ohio, is a remnant of the once vast Black Swamp. Within its borders is a virgin woodland, characterized by huge oaks, beech and ash trees. A few of these giants date back to the 15th Century. Moist areas harbor red maple, silver maple and black ash and six species of fern thrive within these shaded depressions . A dense pine plantation spreads across the northern half of the preserve.

The Ohio Department of Natural Resources publishes an excellent guide to Goll Woods, illustrating the plant and animal species that inhabit the forest. Resident wildlife includes white-tailed deer, red fox, barred owls, red squirrels, red-headed woodpeckers, wood frogs and the rare spotted turtle. Representative trees are labled along the **Cottonwood Trail (A)**, assisting your study of these living fossils.

Trail Route:

The Preserve's hiking trails, all well-marked and maintained, radiate from the parking area. The following combined route yields a hike of 3.75 miles and crosses through the varied habitat of the refuge.

From the parking lot, follow the **Cotton-wood Trail (A)** toward the south as it parallels Township Road 26. Bypass the cutoff to the **Tuliptree Trail (D)** and curve eastward through the forest. Known as the East Woods, this area harbors the prime zone of virgin hardwoods. **Cottonwood Trail** completes a 1.75 mile loop through the woodland; use of the **Burr Oak Trail (B)** shortcuts the distance to 1.0 mile.

Completing your loop through the East Woods, return to the parking area, cross Township Road 26 and pick up the **Toad-shade Trail (C)**. After entering the woods, the trail angles to the north and winds through the dense, cool and dark pine forest. Crossing Township Road F, it then leads down to the south bank of the Tiffin River where an overlook yields a view of the stream. Turning westward, the **Toad-shade Trail** parallels the river for a short distance and then cuts into the woods, passing an area of swamp forest. The route re-crosses Road F near the Goll Cemetery, where a plaque commemorates the history of the region, beginning with the arrival of Peter and Catherine Goll from Grand-Charmont, France, in 1836.

The trail leads southward through the pine plantation and then re-enters the hardwood forest. At this point, the **Toadshade Trail** angles to the left (east), skirting a meadow and heading back to the parking lot. Proceed southward on the **Tuliptree Trail (D)** which meanders through the West Woods, crosses Township Road 26 and intersects the **Cottonwood Trail (A)**. Turn left for a short walk back to the parking area.

Directions:

To reach Goll Woods, follow S.R. 66 north from Archbold and drive 1.6 miles. Turn left (west) on Township Road F and proceed 2.8 miles to Township Road 26. Turn left (south) and the Goll Woods parking lot will be .2 mile, on your left.

Crossing the East Woods

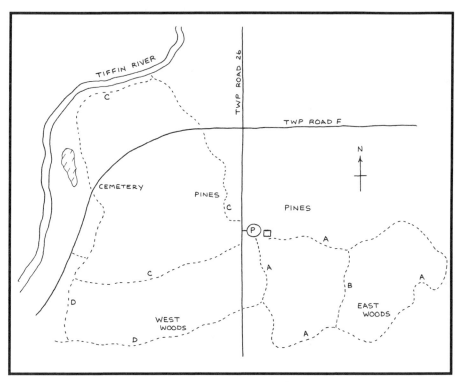

THE GOLL WOODS PRESERVE

2   OAK OPENINGS PRESERVE

Distance: Day hikes of 2.0, 2.5 and 2.9 miles; longer combined routes
Terrain: rolling

The Great Lake basins were scooped from the valleys of an ancient river system as the Wisconsin Glacier plowed into the Midwest, some 70,000 years ago. As the ice retreated into Canada, meltwater and run-off from surrounding uplands created post-glacial lakes that were much larger than those we find today. Lake Warren, predecessor to Lake Erie, extended across what are now the northern counties of Ohio. Eventually, the Lakes spilled to the east via the St. Lawrence River and the water fell to current levels.

Remnant "beaches," sandy soil and unique, "coastal" plant communities attest to the original extent of Lake Warren; the Oak Openings Preserve, one of Toledo's Metroparks, harbors a fine collection of these glacial relics. The Preserve lies within a sandy belt that stretches for twenty-two miles across northwest Ohio. Encompassing the Buehner Walking Center, Oak Openings is accessed by 27 miles of hiking trails, 20 miles of bridal paths and 6 miles of paved bikeways. The map in this guide depicts only the hiking trails.

Trail Routes:

Of the 27 miles of hiking trails, 17 comprise a **Backpack Trail (BPT)** loop, blazed with green markers, that circum-navigates the Preserve. For day hikes, I recommend the routes discussed below; despite numerous intersections with bridal paths and bikeways, the trails are well-marked with colored plaques and easily followed.

Ferns Trail (FT; 2.9 miles). Blazed with dark-blue markers, this trail begins on the east side of the Buehner Walking Center (BWC) and leads northward along Mallard Lake. Cross the inlet channel via a bridge and begin an elongated loop to the north, winding through the moist wood-

land that flanks the stream. Songbirds are abundant in this area and broad-winged hawks are common during the warmer months. Ferns thrive across the cool woodland and wildflowers adorn the valley in April and May.

Sand Dunes Trail (SDT; 2.0 miles). Blazed with red, this loop begins west of the Walking Center parking lot, curving to the north through a forest of white pine. After crossing an abandoned road the path splits into its loop. Sandy soil, open oak woodlands and rolling terrain characterize the route. Dry meadows are carpeted with grassland wildflowers while ferns and swamp maples colonize the moist depressions. At the north end of the loop the trail skirts along Ohio's only inland sand dunes.

Ridge Trail (RT; 2.5 miles). Blazed with silver markers, this trail starts west of the Walking Center lot and cuts to the south, crossing Oak Openings Parkway. It then forks to the left, leaving the **Horseshoe Lake Trail (HLT)** and descends along a side stream to the primary creek channel. Cross the creek and bear right along the loop which stretches atop a low ridge flanking the south wall of the valley. Moist ravines, ferns, hemlocks, big-leaf aspen, tamarack and black oak will be found along north-facing slopes of the ridge. The drier upland forest is characterized by white pine, white oak and black gum trees. Wildflowers, including red trillium, peak from late April through mid May. Wood thrushes seem to be everywhere in summer and barred owls ask "Who cooks for you?" throughout the year. Completing the loop, return to the Walking Center via the entry trail.

The above routes can obviously be combined to yield longer hikes. The **Horseshoe Lake Trail (HLT; 1.4 miles; yellow markers)** and the **Evergreen Trail**

*The remnant
dunes of
Lake Warren.*

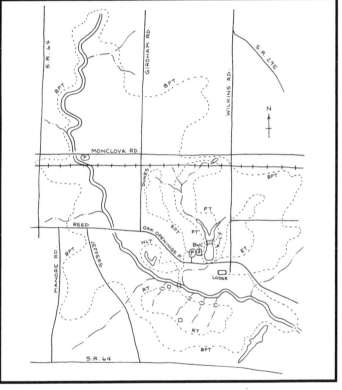

OAK OPENINGS PRESERVE

(ET; 2.0 miles; orange markers) are illustrated on the map but were not researched for this guide. The **Lake Trail (LT; light blue markers)** is a .5 mile loop around Mallard Lake.

Directions:
From I-475, on the west side of metro Toledo, take the Exit for S.R. 2 and drive west. Proceed 8 miles and turn left (south) on S.R. 295. Drive .4 mile, bear right onto Wilkins Road and continue southward for 2.4 miles. Turn right (west) on Oak Openings Parkway and proceed .3 mile to the Mallard Lake/Buehner Walking Center lot, on your right.

3 MAUMEE RIVER PARKS

Distance: Day hikes of 3.4 and 12.5 miles
Terrain: flat

A hike along the north bank of the Maumee River offers a pleasant mix of history and natural scenery. The **Towpath Trail (TPT)**, also a segment of the **Buckeye Trail (BT)**, follows the abandoned channel of the Miami & Erie Canal. The Canal, completed in 1845, was used to transport cargo between the Great Lakes and the Ohio River. Activity on the waterway peaked in the mid 1800s but soon dwindled as railroads invaded "the West." By 1900, use of the Canal was restricted to local commerce.

The **Ludwig Mill (LM)**, built in 1846, is still in use today. Within this historic structure water-driven turbines power a sawmill and a flour mill. Named after Isaac Ludwig, a regional canal boat builder who purchased the Mill in 1865, the facility is open to the public from May through October, noon to 5 PM, Wednesday through Sunday. Admission is free.

The 8-mile **Towpath Trail** connects three of the Toledo Metroparks, extending from **Providence Dam** to the **Farnsworth Metropark**. Since a 16 mile roundtrip stroll would challenge even the most avid walker, the following day hikes are suggested.

Trail Routes:

A. Providence Metropark to Bend View Park (12.5 miles roundtrip). Bend View Park is a popular destination for day hikes. While it offers broad views of the Maumee River, the Park is accessed only by canoe or foot trail, ensuring some seclu-sion from the picnic crowds. Though the hiking distance is long, flat terrain makes the going easy and wildlife is abundant along the way. Watch for white-tailed deer, raccoons and wood ducks along the abandoned Canal.

Providence Metropark is adjacent to the **Providence Dam**, which diverts water to the **Ludwig Mill**, .5 mile downstream. Be sure to visit the Mill before of after your hike.

B. Farnsworth Metropark to Bend View Park (3.4 miles roundtrip). Starting at **Farnsworth Metropark** and hiking westward along the **Towpath Trail**, one can reach **Bend View Park** with its relative seclusion and sweeping views in just under 1.7 miles. As an added attraction, **Roche De Boeuf (ROB)**, at the west edge of **Farnsworth**, is a scenic swath of rapids where gulls, shorebirds and herons often come to feed. After a picnic lunch at **Bend View**, return to your car via the same route.

Directions:

The Toledo Metroparks discussed above all lie in a narrow band between U.S. 24 and the Maumee River. From I-475, on the southwest side of Toledo, take the U.S. 24 Exit and drive southwest through the Maumee River Valley. Farnsworth Metropark will be approximately 2 miles west of Waterville. Providence Metropark and the Ludwig Mill are just west of the U.S. 24/S.R. 578 junction.

Winter on the Maumee

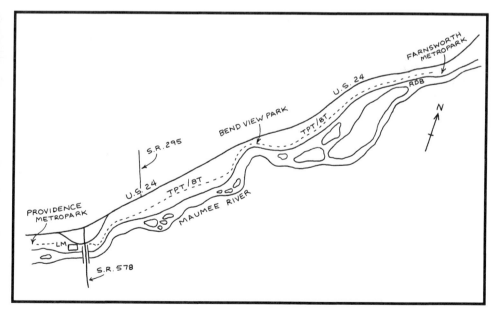

THE TOWPATH TRAIL

4 MIAMI & ERIE TRAIL

Distance: Day hikes of 4.0, 4.4, 5.0, 6.0, 10.4 and 12.0 miles
Terrain: flat

The Miami & Erie Canal, completed in 1845, stretched from Toledo to Cincinnati. Its 266 miles of waterway, controlled by 105 locks, provided an important avenue for cargo transport in western Ohio. Five feeder lakes, including Lake Loramie and Grand Lake St. Marys, were constructed to ensure a steady flow of water through the Canal.

The emergence of railroads in the mid 1800s led to the demise of Canal traffic by the end of the Century. Since then, much of the Canal has been obliterated by paved roads and urban construction. To preserve a piece of Canal history the 40-mile **Miami & Erie Trail** was created under the Ohio Trails Act and now follows the abandoned towpath of the Canal. The Trail stretches from Lake Loramie State Park northward to Delphos, Ohio; its route is utilized by a section of the **Buckeye Trail.**

The 8-mile stretch south of Spencerville is open to horseback riders and the 9-mile section north of St. Marys is watered and open to canoeists. The map in this guide is limited to the 13-mile portion from St. Marys to Spencerville, including the above two segments, and covers what is perhaps the most scenic part of the Trail. The following day hikes are suggested.

Trail Routes:

Deep Cut Park to Bloody Bridge (10.4 miles roundtrip). Park at Deep Cut Park, on the west side of S.R. 66, approximately 2 miles south of Spencerville. This small Park stretches above the greatest excavation that was undertaken during construction of the Miami & Erie Canal. Five to fifty-two feet deep and 6600 feet long, the trench cuts through a ridge that separates the watersheds of the St. Marys and Auglaize Rivers. Walk southward above the old channel and cross the bridge to the abandoned towpath that paralleled the west bank of the Canal.

Hike to the south and then curve eastward, crossing S.R. 66. After hiking about 2.2 miles you will reach the town of Kossuth and from here to St. Marys the Canal is kept watered for sightseers and canoeists. Another 3 miles of walking brings you to Bloody Bridge where a plaque along the Trail describes the incident that gave the bridge its name.

Bloody Bridge to Feeder Pond (5 miles roundtrip). A small, gravel lot sits along the east side of S.R. 66, approximately 5 miles north of U.S. 33. This is the Bloody Bridge access point for the **Miami & Erie Trail.** Hike southward along the old towpath, cross S.R. 66 and continue across the farmlands of Auglaize County. After hiking approximately 2.5 miles you will see a 40 acre pond, east of the Canal, that formerly served as a turn-around and feeder lake. After a respite near the pond, retrace your route to Bloody Bridge.

Other possible day hikes include:
Bloody Bridge to Kossuth
    (6 miles roundtrip)
Deep Cut to Kossuth
    (4.4 miles roundtrip)
St. Marys to Bloody Bridge
    (12 miles roundtrip)
Deep Cut to Spencerville
    (4 miles roundtrip)

Directions:

From I-75 at Wapakoneta, take Exit #110 and drive west on U.S. 33 for approximately 12 miles to S.R. 66. Turn north to Bloody Bridge, Kossuth, Deep Cut Park or Spencerville (as illustrated on the map) or south to St. Marys. The most convenient access point in St. Marys is at Geiger Park, on the south end of town.

16

The Canal just south of Deep Cut Park.

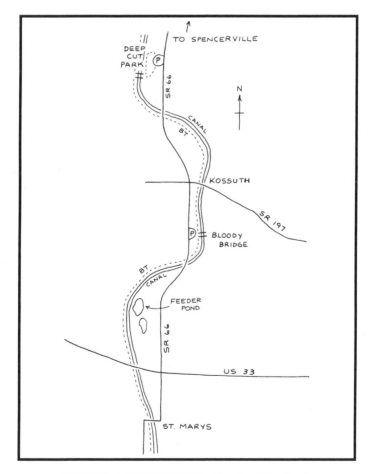

MIAMI & ERIE TRAIL (Central Section)

5 LAKE LORAMIE STATE PARK

Distance: 4.5 miles roundtrip
Terrain: flat

Lake Loramie is a 1655 acre reservoir in western Ohio. Constructed in the 1840s, it was one of five "feeder lakes" for the Miami-Erie Canal (see Hikes 3 and 4).

Lake Loramie State Park now stretches along the western shores of the reservoir. Popular for camping, fishing and boating, the Park also offers a unique hiking experience. For the naturalist, the wetlands in and around the Park support one of the northernmost stands of baldcypress trees in the United States. Birdwatchers will enjoy the large populations of Canada geese and great blue herons, in addition to numerous migrants during the spring and fall.

Trail Route:

The **Blackberry Island Trail** combines a 1.5 mile hike from Ft. Loramie-Swanders Road to the Island footbridge with a 1.5 mile loop around the Island itself. The total roundtrip distance is thus 4.5 miles.

Park in the small lot just off S.R. 362, on the west side of the Lake's south inlet (see map). Walk south along the lagoon, ascend to Ft. Loramie-Swanders Road and turn left (east), crossing the bridge. Approximately 10 yards east of the bridge, turn north onto a gravel jeep trail that cuts through the field along the inlet. The first section is often indistinct and obscured by vegetation during the summer months. Find your way northward through the field, staying close to the lagoon and watching for sinkholes along the way.

Once at the north end of the field, turn right and follow the wide, grassy trail that parallels another inlet channel. Hike approximately 1/3 mile and then loop around

the eastern end of the lagoon, veering northward into the forest. The trail winds along the edge of this woodland, eventually curving to the east. Drainage from adjacent crop fields can produce boggy conditions along this section of the hike. Views of Lake Loramie and of Blackberry Island begin to unfold on your left. You will finally emerge into a clearing where rusting construction equipment sits along a graveled loop.

Walk to the north end of the clearing and follow the broad path that leads out to the Island's footbridge. Cross the bridge, walk approximately 50 yards and angle to the right or left, following the loop trail around Blackberry Island. The trail remains in the forest for most of its route and views of the Lake are best obtained at either end of the loop. Filburn's Island, actually a peninsula, lies east of Blackberry Island and harbors a small residential community. Blackberry Island itself is split by a central channel; the trail loops around the eastern half of the Island.

After completing the Island circuit, return to the parking area via the same route.

Directions:

To reach Lake Loramie State Park, take Exit #93 (St. Mary-Sidney Exit) from I-75 and follow S.R. 29 northwest for 4 miles. Turn left (west) on Ft. Loramie-Swanders Road and drive 6.9 miles across a rolling countryside of silos and dairy farms. Turn right onto S.R. 362 and take an immediate right into the picnic area along the Lake's south inlet. Park here and pick up the trail as described above.

Footbridge to the Island

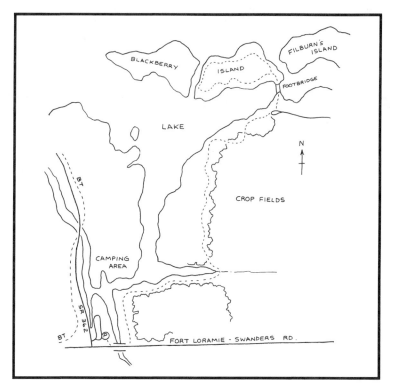

TRAIL TO BLACKBERRY ISLAND

6 STILLWATER PRAIRIE RESERVE

Distance: 2.0 miles
Terrain: rolling

Grass is a relative newcomer to the plant kingdom. While ferns and conifers hail from the mid Paleozoic Era, grasses evolved approximately 25-30 million years ago in the rain shadow of the young Rocky Mountains. More tolerant of cold, wind and drought, prairie grasslands began to replace forests in the central longitudes of North America and, by the arrival of the first white pioneers, a "sea of grass" stretched from western Ohio to the foot of the Rockies. Tolerance to wildfire, quick recovery from the trampling and grazing of buffalo and the grassland's ability to deprive tree seedlings of vital light and water, all favored expansion of the prairie.

Today, only a few small remnants of the tallgrass prairie persist in western Ohio. Though never extensive in our State, most of the original grassland has succumbed to the farmer's plow. Stillwater Prairie Reserve, in Miami County, protects a small relict prairie that has survived man's assault on the landscape.

The 217 acre preserve, stretching for one mile along the Stillwater River, is the former site of a sawmill, operated by the Hagan family during the 1840's. The land was acquired by the Miami County Park District during the late 1970's. Access to the Reserve is via a 2 mile network of trails and boardwalks.

Trail Route:

From the east parking lot, follow the boardwalk as it winds southward through a parcel of mature forest. At the trail intersection, bear left and descend onto the floodplain of the Stillwater River, where the relict prairie flanks both sides of the stream. Angle left onto the boardwalk that curves through the prairie. Big and little bluestem typify the grassland and prairie wildflowers abound from mid to late summer. If water conditions permit, cross the river to complete a loop through the prairie that lies south of the Stillwater's channel.

Return to the main trail which follows the river upstream. At the western end of this section, a plaque commemorates the designation of the Stillwater as a State Scenic River, on October 14, 1980. The trail turns northward, crossing open fields along a boardwalk. White-tail deer are often spotted here and turkey vultures roost along the western edge of this grassland from March through October. Bear right at the trail fork, soon winding past the old Hagan homestead (circa 1846). Angle eastward, ascending from the floodplain.

Turn left at the next trail intersection and loop around the Reserve's marsh-lined pond. Small docks along the shore service fishermen and nature-watchers. Return to the intersection and turn left, descending and then climbing through an open woodland. Re-entering the forest, bear left onto the entry trail and return to the parking area.

Directions:

Stillwater Prairie Reserve stretches along the south side of S.R. 185, 8.5 miles west of Piqua (1.5 miles west of the intersection with route 48). The Reserve is open all year from dawn to dusk. There is no entry fee.

Crossing the Prairie

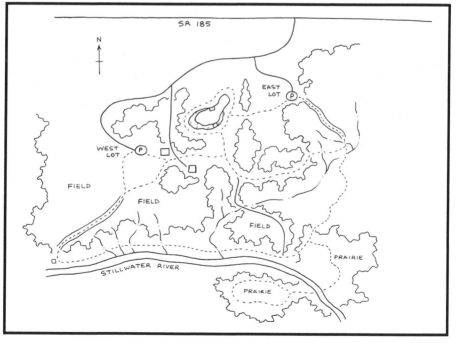

STILLWATER PRAIRIE PRESERVE

7 ENGLEWOOD RESERVE

Distance: 3.25 miles
Terrain: rolling; few hilly areas

Englewood Reserve, characterized by 1282 acres of forest, meadow and wetlands, is the largest nature preserve in the Dayton-Montgomery County Park District. Despite its proximity to a large metropolitan area, the Reserve is exceptionally clean and well maintained. In addition, the District's attention to minimizing impact on the natural environment has ensured that the visitor will experience an excellent diversity of wildlife and habitat.

Construction of the Englewood Dam, in 1952, diverted the Stillwater River into adjacent lowlands, creating East Lake. Slowly filling with sediment, the Lake is ringed by marsh, swamp forest and wet meadows. Herons, waterfowl and other marshland residents attract naturalists throughout the year.

Numerous trails and bridal paths wind through the Reserve. The following 3.25 mile hike will take you through varied habitats and past some of Englewood's more scenic areas.

Trail Route:

Park in one of the lots at the north end of East Lake (see map). A trail leads westward from the parking area, crossing between the Lake and a backwater marsh. Reaching a fork in the trail, bear left and continue along the Lake's northern shore. Upon reaching the banks of the Stillwater River, the trail angles to the right (north) and heads upstream. Since the trail runs atop the bank, usually 8-10 feet above the water's surface, the path is generally easy to traverse. However, heavy rains or high river levels can produce boggy conditions along this section of the hike.

Continue northward along the scenic stream for approximately ¾ mile. The trail then turns to the right and gently ascends through the hillside forest. About ¼ mile up

the ridge, the trail begins a steep climb and soon reaches an intersection. Turn left and hike along the valley wall. The trail undulates northward for ½ mile, crossing numerous drainage channels. At its terminus the visitor is treated to a view of Martindale Falls (1), which plunges from the ridgetop into a wide ravine.

Ascend the short stairway that climbs higher along the ridge and angle to the right (south) along a flat, rocky trail. During the winter months, extensive views of the Stillwater Valley open to the west. Hike ½ mile and turn left (east) at the trail intersection. Entering a remnant swamp forest, the trail is elevated along a boardwalk. A side trail leads out to a stand of pumpkin ash trees (2), a threatened species in Ohio.

Continue southward along the main trail, passing two trails that lead off to the right. You will eventually arrive at Patty's Falls (3), crossing the stream above the cascade. Angle to the right and descend to the Falls overlook where a plaque describes the geologic features of this area. Proceed downhill along a deep ravine and cross under the roadway. Angle up to the road and hike westward for ½ mile to the parking area. Your hike through the Reserve has totalled 3.25 miles.

You may wish to add another .75 mile to your route by circling around the backwater marsh, just north of the parking area. For those who prefer a shorter hike, the Reserve offers a .75 mile, self-guided nature trail (NT). Brochures are provided at the trailhead along Patty's Road (see map).

Directions:

Take Exit #63 from I-75 (2 miles north of I-70). Turn west on U.S. 40 and drive 5 miles. The entrance to Englewood Reserve will be on your right, just before you cross the Dam. Follow the roadway as it winds into the Stillwater Valley and bear right along the eastern shore of the Lake. Proceed to the parking areas north of East Lake. There is no entrance fee.

Summer along the Stillwater

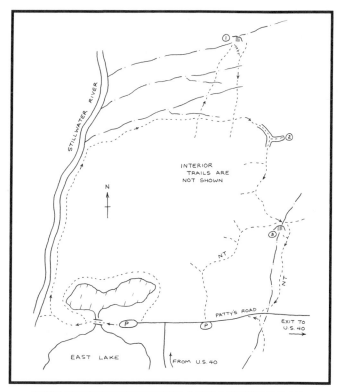

THE RESERVE NORTH OF PATTY'S ROAD

8 AULLWOOD AUDUBON CENTER & FARM

Distance: 2.3 miles
Terrain: rolling

The Aullwood Audubon Center & Farm, northwest of Dayton, is the National Audubon Society's education center for the Great Lakes Region. Donated by Mrs. John Aull, the 200 acre preserve was dedicated in 1957.

A network of wide, well-marked trails radiate into the sanctuary from the Aullwood education building. The latter houses the Center's offices, a nature-oriented bookstore and an exhibit hall. The extensive trail system offers a variety of routes through the preserve; the following route maximizes your walking distance and winds through the various habitats that characterize the refuge.

Trail Route:

Start behind the education building and walk to the south, following the trail that heads toward Bluegill Pond. Wind downstream along Aullwood Brook, soon passing a broad meadow on your right. Bypass the cutoff to the Fossil Beds, cross the creek and ascend a short stairway, emerging from the woods along the north shore of Bluegill Pond.

Hike eastward, bearing right at the fork in the trail, and follow the path to the Wet Woods. Circle through the Woods (see map) and re-emerge along Aullwood's central prairie. This reconstructed grassland is characterized by big bluestem and prairie dock. Hike northward along the eastern edge of the prairie, soon intersecting the course of Aullwood's **Discovery Trail (DT)**; at this intersection, a connecting trail leads eastward to the Big Spring Area of the Englewood Reserve. Rising above the intersection, an observation tower (T) provides an overview of the grassland which is adorned with wildflowers during the summer months.

Continue northward along the **Discovery Trail**, entering the forest. Bear right at the next three intersections, leaving the **Discovery Trail** at the third fork. Climbing higher and proceeding toward the Farm area, bypass the cutoff to the Pasture (on your right). You will soon arrive at an observation blind (B) that sits next to a small drainage pond. Continuing northward, another ¼ mile hike takes you out of the forest, across an open pasture and into the heart of Aullwood's Farm.

The working Farm at Aullwood is designed to expose the visitor to the interrelationship between nature and man's agricultural activities. Too often, we urbanites take for granted the vital work of our rural brethren and, just as blindly, ignore the impact of their practices on the health of our natural environment.

After soaking in the sights, sounds and smells of the Farm, return to the observation blind (B) and turn to the west along the **Shawnee Trail (ST)**. This narrow path winds downhill, following a sidestream of Aullwood Brook, and cuts through a dense, immature woodland. Entering the Northwoods area, the route merges with the **Discovery Trail (DT)**. Bypass the first cutoff on your right, parallel Aullwood Brook for a short distance and then curve to the right, crossing the stream.

A short boardwalk takes you across a boggy area and the trail then angles to the south, heading toward Muskrat Marsh. Another boardwalk just north of the Marsh leads into a Wet Meadow which is dominated by scouring rush. During the warmer months, look for showy lady's slipper, fringed gentian, turtlehead, Michigan lily and other unusual plants in the meadow.

Continue southward along the **Discovery Trail**, merging with the **Brush Hill Loop (BH)**, and return to the education center. Your hike through the Aullwood Center and Farm has totalled 2.3 miles.

*Aullwood's
Prairie
Habitat*

AULLWOOD
AUDUBON CENTER
& FARM

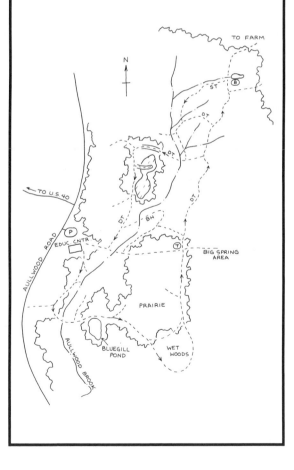

Directions:

Take Exit #63 from I-75 (2 miles north of I-70). Turn west on U.S. 40 and drive 5 miles. The entry road to the Center will be on your left, just before crossing the Englewood Dam. Admission is currently $2.00 per adult and $1.00 per child; admission is free for Audubon Society members. The Center is open 9 a.m. to 5 p.m., Mon.-Sat., and 1-5 p.m. on Sunday.

9 CHARLESTON FALLS PRESERVE

Distance: 3.0 miles
Terrain: rolling; few stairways

Plunging 37 feet into a narrow limestone gorge, Charleston Falls is the highest cascade in western Ohio. To protect this scenic resource, the Miami County Park District, in concert with the Nature Conservancy and the George Gund Foundation, has established a 169 acre nature preserve bordering the course of Charleston Creek. Access to the Preserve's varied habitat is provided by a fine network of trails and boardwalks. The following route yields a 3 mile hike through this scenic refuge.

Trail Route:

From the parking lot, walk eastward into the woods. Turn left, hike a short distance and bear right onto the **Falls Trail (A)**. A .3 mile walk through the forest will bring you to an overlook (1) on the south edge of the gorge. After enjoying the view, continue eastward on the **Falls Trail**, curving behind and above the falls and crossing Charleston Creek. Bear right onto the **Thorny Badlands Trail (B)** which dips across another branch of the creek and ascends into a pine plantation. Angling westward, the trail soon leaves this woodland and crosses an open area where nature is recovering from past cultivation and clear-cutting. An observation tower (2) permits an overview of this area and offers an excellent site for watching resident wildlife.

Continue westward, re-enter the forest and turn left onto the **Redbud Valley Trail (C)**. This trail parallels the creek, crosses a wet meadow via a boardwalk and then climbs onto the north wall of the gorge. At the top of the ridge, angle right onto the **Lower Viewing Trail (D)** which hugs the wall of the gorge, passing a cave (3) in the Silurian limestone. Descend to the creek where a boardwalk crosses the stream and offers a splendid view of Charleston Falls. Note that the more resistant layers of Silurian limestone overlie soft Ordovician shale, predisposing to formation of the falls. During the warmer months, scan the cliffs for wild columbine, purple cliffbreak, rock honeysuckle and walking fern that thrive in the cool, moist recesses of the gorge.

Ascend the south wall of the chasm and turn left, again following the **Falls Trail (A)** as it circles behind the waterfall and crosses Charleston Creek. Bear left onto the **Redbud Valley Trail (C)**, hike westward above the gorge, descend from the ridge and recross the wet meadow on the boardwalk. Turn left onto the **Main Trail (E)** which follows the creek downstream.

Curving to the south, the trail crosses Charleston Creek and emerges onto the Preserve's reconstructed prairie. Bear left onto the **Prairie Trail (F)**, a narrow path that cuts through the grassland and permits close study of its varied plantlife. Turn left on the **Main Trail** and then left onto a short spur loop, the **Pond Trail (G)**, that leads down to the Preserve's man-made pond. Created in 1977, the pond is ringed by a marsh that will slowly spread toward the center as sediments accumulate on the floor of the basin. Swallows skim above the surface during the warmer months while herons stalk the cattails for minnows and frogs. Deer, raccoons and opossums may be spotted along the banks throughout the year.

After a respite above the pond, return to the **Main Trail (E)**, turn left and hike back to the parking area.

Directions:

Follow I-70 to Exit 36 (3 miles east of I-75). Turn north on Ohio 202 and drive 3.2 miles. Turn left (west) on Ross Road and proceed .9 mile to the Preserve, on your right.

*Charleston
Falls*

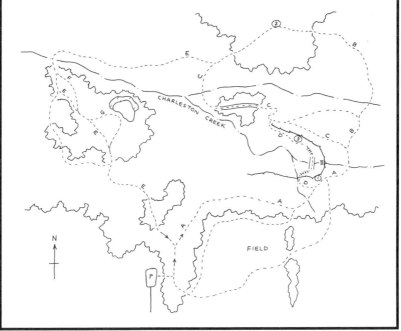

CHARLESTON FALLS PRESERVE

10 HIGHBANKS METRO PARK

Distance: Day hikes of 1.0, 4.5 and 5.5 miles
Terrain: rolling; few steep areas and stairways

Named for its perch above the east bank of the Olentangy River, Highbanks Metro Park, north of Columbus, offers excellent hiking through scenic terrain. Deep ravines slice through the forested slopes of the valley wall and the Park's wide, even trails lead through a fine diversity of habitat.

Designated a National Natural Landmark, the southern section of the Park has been set aside as a Nature Preserve and it is here that the "high banks" are most impressive. Composed primarily of Ohio Shale, deposited in Devonian seas some 335 million years ago, the cliffs are topped by glacial till left behind by the Wisconsin Ice Sheet. The rich till supports a mixed forest of beech, oak and hickory across the ridgetops while elm, ash and maples cluster along the moist ravines.

The Park's 6-mile network of hiking trails consists of five interconnected loops. The routes are well-engineered, skirting the deep ravines and providing broad vistas along the way. There are few steep areas and even the inexperienced hiker will have little trouble traversing the paths. A fine collection of rustic bridges carry the visitor across the Park's many streams. The following 4.5 mile hike is suggested.

Trail Route:
Entering the Park from U.S. 23, drive .4 mile and bear left toward the Nature Center/Ranger Station and the Oak Coves Picnic Area. Park in one of the first two lots on your right. Hike eastward and pick up the **Dogwood Trail (D)** on the south side of the entry road (see map). Enter the forest and veer to the left, soon crossing the first of many bridges. The trail curves back to the west, following high ground between two ravines. Bear left at the next fork,

switching to the **Old Orchard Trail (C)** and crossing another stream.

Proceed .2 mile and turn left onto the **Overlook Trail (E)**. This route leads across an open meadow, dips through two ravines and then splits into a loop. Turn right onto the loop and you will soon cross a deep gorge via a long, wooden bridge. Just before reaching the south end of the loop you will notice a low, earthen wall on your right. This is the remnant of a prehistoric Indian mound, dating back some 2000 years, which probably enclosed a ceremonial "fortress" above the high banks of the Olentangy.

At the end of the loop, angle westward to the Overlook, cutting across the mound and its adjacent moat. A short walk brings you to a bluff-top deck overlooking the River, its floodplain and the shale cliffs discussed above. The vista is most impressive during the colder months when leaves have dropped to the forest floor.

Backtrack to the loop, bear right and return to the **Old Orchard Trail (C)**. Turn left, cross the bridge and ascend along a parking area. Continue westward along the **Dripping Rock Trail (B)** which winds above a deep ravine, crosses a sidestream and then curves northward above the Olentangy River. Tunneling under the Park road, the trail continues to the north where it intersects an entry path from the Big Meadows Picnic Area.

Bear right, crossing the bridge and proceed a short distance to another fork in the trail. Bear right again, ascending into the forest via a stairway. Leading eastward, the **Dripping Rock Trail** meanders above the Park's most impressive ravine, crossing numerous sidestreams and curving near the rim of the gorge at several points. After fording the primary creek via the Arch Bridge, the trail climbs to the Park's

28

Highbanks Park has many scenic bridges.

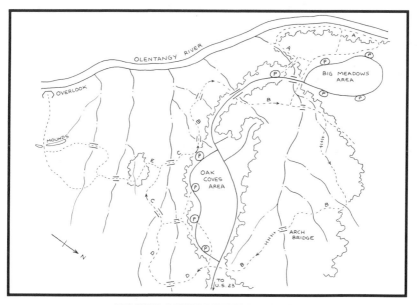

HIGHBANKS METRO PARK

central roadway near the turnoff to Oak Coves.

As an addition to the above route, or as a separate hike, the **Olentangy Loop Trail (A)** provides a 1-mile stroll across flat terrain. Paralleling the River for much of its course, this loop crosses through riparian woodland and streamside meadows. Wildflowers are abundant along the trail from April through September.

Directions:

From I-270, north of Columbus, take Exit #23 and drive north on U.S. 23. Proceed 2.7 miles to the Park entrance, on your left. Parking areas are shown on the map.

III. HIKING AREAS OF NORTH-CENTRAL OHIO

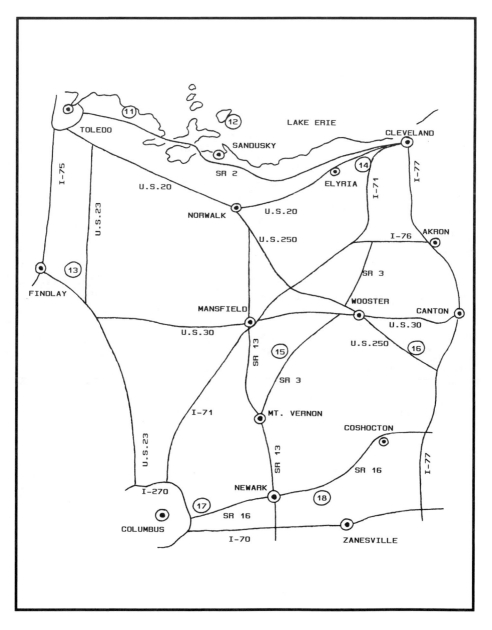

HIKING AREAS OF NORTH-CENTRAL OHIO

11 OTTAWA NATIONAL WILDLIFE REFUGE

Distance: 4.2 miles
Terrain: flat

There are few sights in nature more stirring than the graceful but noisy assemblage of a huge flock of tundra swans. Such an experience can be enjoyed at Ottawa National Wildlife Refuge, on the southwest shore of Lake Erie, during the spring and fall migrations. These magnificent birds winter along the mid-Atlantic coast and utilize the Ottawa wetlands during their journey to and from their Arctic breeding grounds. Their numbers at the refuge generally peak from mid March to early April.

The 5800 acres of Ottawa National Wildlife Refuge protect a small remnant of the once vast marshland that stretched along the southern shore of Lake Erie. Most of the wetland has since succumbed to drainage and pollution and the Refuge, established in 1961, has become a vital link in the migratory route of numerous shorebirds and waterfowl. Ottawa offers nesting habitat for many of these waterbirds in addition to herons, egrets and a tremendous variety of songbirds. Bald eagles and ospreys utilize the Preserve and resident mammals include white-tailed deer, woodchucks, muskrats, red fox and raccoons.

A seven-mile trail network runs atop flood control dikes and provides access to the Refuge for birdwatchers and hikers. Wind is a constant companion across these flat, open wetlands and its chilling effect is noticable even during the summer months; proper clothing is advised. In addition, insect repellent is imperative during the spring and summer. The following route yields a 4.2 mile hike and crosses through the sub-habitats within the Preserve.

Trail Route:

From the parking lot, adjacent to the Refuge Office, hike northward on the **Blue Heron Trail**, blazed with blue markers. Flooding of the cropland, on your left, attracts geese, surface-feeding ducks and

shorebirds during the spring migration. Continue northward on sections of the **Swan Loop** (blazed with white markers) and the **Yellow Legs Loop** (yellow markers), eventually curving to the west along the south bank of Crane Creek. The marshlands within the **Swan, Yellowlegs** and **Mallard Loops** attract a wide variety of waterfowl, shorebirds, herons, egrets and songbirds, especially from March through November. Loons, gulls, diving ducks and pelagic species favor the deeper waters of Lake Erie.

Hike westward for 1.2 miles and loop back to the east via the **Mallard Trail** (blazed with green markers). Turn south along the west side of the **Swan Loop** and then turn right (west) on the **Blue Heron Trail**. You will soon enter a parcel of swamp forest, a remnant of the great Black Swamp that covered much of northwestern Ohio after the Pleistocene. Since most of these woodlands have been cleared for farming, the islands of forest that remain fill with songbirds during the spring and fall migrations. Confronted by the vast stretch of water to the north, spring warblers congregate here to feed and rest up before attempting to cross Lake Erie.

Wind through the forest and then angle eastward along the **Blue Heron Trail**. Bypass the trail's southern excursion, staying on the south edge of the crop field. Emerging onto the Preserve's entry road, turn left and return to the parking lot.

Directions:

Ottawa National Wildlife Refuge lies north of S.R. 2, 15 miles east of Toledo (or 18 miles west of Port Clinton). A bird checklist (covering 267 species) and other information regarding the Refuge can be obtained by writing to the address listed in Appendix II.

Winter Scene at the Refuge

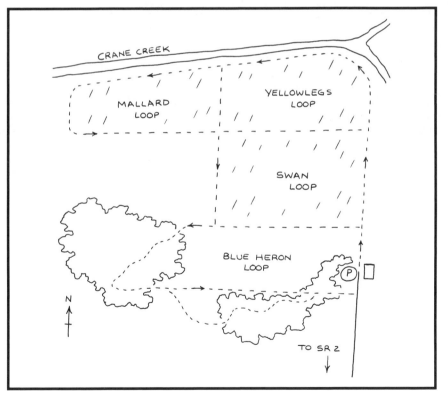

OTTAWA NATIONAL WILDLIFE REFUGE

12 KELLEYS ISLAND

Distance: 9.0 miles
Terrain: flat; few gentle hills

Kelleys Island is the largest of Ohio's Lake Erie islands. Capped by resistant Columbus limestone, which was deposited in Devonian seas, this archipelago was left behind after the Wisconsin glacier scoured out the Great Lake basins and then retreated into Canada. Human settlement began soon thereafter as Paleo-hunters arrived in the area. The Island is named for Datus and Ira Kelley who purchased it in the 1830s to quarry its rich supply of limestone. A relatively mild climate, moderated by the waters of Lake Erie, proved to be ideal for vineyards and small wineries dotted the Island during the late 1800s.

A nine mile hike across Kelleys Island provides an appealing blend of natural beauty and human history.

Trail Route:

Park on the mainland at the Neuman Boat Line lot in Marblehead (see Directions) and cross the 4.5 mile channel to Kelleys Island via the ferry. From the Island port, walk eastward along **Water St.** to the village center. Attractive lakefront homes and views of the channel highlight this .8 mile stretch. Once in town, stock up on snacks and drinks before heading north along **Division St.** Cutting through the center of the Island, this avenue is lined with 19th Century homes and old, historic churches. Incorporated in 1887, the Village is listed in the National Register of Historic Places.

Pass Chapel St., Bookerman Road and Ward Road and cross to the east side of **Division St.** at the Village Cemetery (C), continuing north along the sidewalk. Another .25 mile takes you past the State Park Campgrounds and out to the **Glacial Grooves State Memorial (GG)**. This small preserve, a National Natural Landmark, bears testament to the erosive force of the Pleistocene glaciers. The massive ice sheets

and their cargo of igneous rock gouged these grooves into the less-resistant limestone that caps the Island. Unearthed during quarry activity, the grooves are world-renowned for their stark depiction of glacial power.

After looping around the Glacial Grooves, hike northward through a picnic area (P.A.) and follow the gravel road to the west (see map). Bear left at the fork, passing behind an old dock structure and turn right onto the **North Loop Trail (NLT)**. This path winds down to the Lake, turns westward along the shore and then curves back to the southeast, re-emerging along the old quarry road. Spur trails lead down to the rocky, north shore, offering a scenic spot for lunch.

Re-cross the picnic area and follow **Division St.** southward to **Ward Road.** Turn left (east) and hike .7 mile to a small lot on the south side of the road; this is the trailhead for the **East Quarry Area Trails** of Kelleys Island State Park. Trails in the preserve are marked with green **(G)** and orange **(O)** metal plates at trail intersections. Loop around the east end of the remnant quarry lake. Bald eagles and ospreys may be spotted here, scanning the clear waters for fish.

Once on the south side of the lake, proceed westward and bypass two orange trails. Turn left on the green trail, a wide path that leads southward through cedar glades and open woodlands. Bypass all cutoff and crossing trails and continue straight ahead to **Woodford Road.** Turn left and walk .1 mile along the road to the **Kelleys Island Wine Company (W)**, which revived wine making on the Island in 1986. An outdoor wine garden offers welcome refreshment on warm summer days.

Proceed west on **Woodford Road** and turn left on **Addison Road.** The **Kelleys Mansion (M)**, constructed with native limestone in 1863, overlooks the Channel at **Addison** and **Lake Shore Roads.** Across the street, along the south shore of Kelleys Island, is the **Inscription Rock State**

The Glacial Grooves

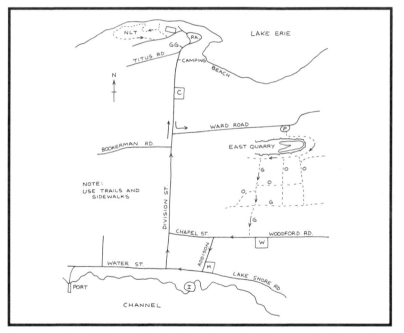

KELLEYS ISLAND

Memorial (I). Carved in limestone, these Erie Indian pictographs date back to the 1600s.

Hike westward along **Water St.** and return to the Neuman Boat Dock, completing a 9 mile walking tour of Kelleys Island.
Directions:

From Port Clinton, drive west on S.R. 163 into Marblehead. The Neuman Boat Line will be on your left as you descend into town. Ferry service is provided hourly during the day from April to mid-November. Half-hour service is provided on summer weekends. For information, contact Neuman Boat Line at 101 E. Shoreline Drive, Sandusky, Ohio, 44870.

13 SPRINGVILLE MARSH STATE NATURE PRESERVE

Distance: 1 mile
Terrain: flat

Springville Marsh State Nature Preserve offers a short hike through a fascinating area. The 160 acre Preserve is a remnant of the Big Spring Prairie which covered much of northwestern Ohio after the Wisconsin Ice Sheets receded into Canada. The combination of flat terrain and abundant ground water created a vast wetland, most of which has since succumbed to encroaching woodland and the farmer's plow.

Springville Marsh, four miles north of Carey, Ohio, was purchased through the assistance of the Nature Conservancy in 1978 and transferred to the care of the Ohio Department of Natural Resources in 1981. A one mile trail, most of which is elevated along a boardwalk, winds through the various sub-habitats of the wetland.

Trail Route:

From the parking area hike southward across the marsh. Cat-tails predominate but patches of twig rush, a native of the Atlantic Coastal Plain, are also found in this unique refuge. Rare species such as Kalm's lobelia, shrubby cinquefoil, bottle gentian and fen orchids may be spotted along the trail. Marshland residents include soras, herons, mink, weasels and the spotted turtle, a threatened species in our State.

The boardwalk crosses an area of phragmites (1), veers to the east and then turns southward again, crossing a peninsula of willow and shrubby dogwood (2). At the trail intersection, bear left and cross through a sedge meadow (3) before reaching an observation blind (4). The ponds before you teem with waterfowl during the spring and fall migrations.

Backtrack to the intersection and turn left. Another spur trail leads out to a tower (5) which offers a panoramic view of the refuge. Return to the main trail loop and turn left, hiking westward across the boardwalk. After entering a moist woodland of hackberry, cottonwood and maple, the trail ascends to slightly higher ground and turns to the north, following the western border of the Preserve. White-tailed deer and red fox may be spotted in this area. Continuing northward, the trail soon angles to the right and returns to the parking lot.

Directions:

From Carey, Ohio, drive north on U.S. 23 for approximately 4 miles. Turn left (west) on Township Road #24. Proceed 1 mile and watch for the parking area, on your left.

Late Winter at the Marsh

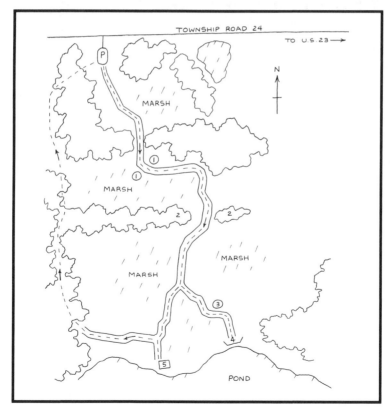

SPRINGVILLE MARSH PRESERVE

14 ROCKY RIVER RESERVATION

Distance: 7.5 miles roundtrip
Terrain: flat to rolling along River; hilly with stairways at Nature Center

Cleveland's superb network of Metro-parks rings the periphery of Cuyahoga County, forming what is known as the "Emerald Necklace." The western rim of the system is formed by the Rocky River Reservation which stretches for over 15 miles along the River and its Eastern Branch. Up to a mile wide, the Reservation encompasses 5600 acres and is accessed by a Parkway, a paved bike trail and an earthen bridal path, all of which intertwine and parallel the course of the River.

The following 7.5 mile roundtrip hike winds through the central portion of the Reservation and includes some of the Park's more scenic areas.

Trail Route:

Park at the **Berea Falls Overlook (1)** off Barrett Road (see Directions). Presented to the Metropark System by the Kiwanis Club of Cleveland in 1986, the wooden deck offers a spectacular view of Berea Falls. After enjoying the vista, hike northward above the west rim of the gorge. For the next 2.5 miles, wind downstream using either the bridal path or the paved bikeway. These avenues follow the course of the Parkway, crossing and re-crossing the East Branch of Rocky River before reaching Cedar Point Road. To avoid congestion, I decided not to differentiate these two trails on the map; you will likely switch from one to the other along the way since they alternate in their proximity to the River. At stream crossings, especially during spring, you will be forced to use the bikeway bridges.

Cross Cedar Point Road and follow the bike path northeastward through an open picnic area and across the River. Turn left into the **Rocky River Nature Center** and proceed to the **Interpretive Building (2)**. Exhibits depict the natural history of the Reservation and informative brochures are provided for the Center's trail network.

Pick up the 1.2 mile **Fort Hill Trail (FT)** behind the Interpretive Building and hike westward along a marsh. The latter lies within the abandoned channel of the Rocky River. Blazed with arrowhead markers, the trail soon forks. Bear right and continue along the marshy channel before angling to the southwest and climbing onto Fort Hill via a series of stairways. Atop the ridge, bear right at the trail intersection and wind along the north rim of the Rocky River Valley. Your 90-foot vertical climb is rewarded by spectacular views of the River and its steep cliffs of Devonian age shale. **Prehistoric Indian mounds (3)**, thought to have been ceremonial in nature, will be found at the east end of the ridge.

Descend to the Nature Center and, after a picnic lunch, retrace your route to Berea Falls.

Directions:

Take Exit #235 from I-71 and drive west on Bagley Road. Proceed 2.3 miles, crossing the East Branch of the Rocky River, and turn right (north) on Barrett Road. Drive approximately .5 mile and bear right into the Metropark. The Berea Falls Overlook lot will be on your right.

View of Rocky River from Fort Hill Trail

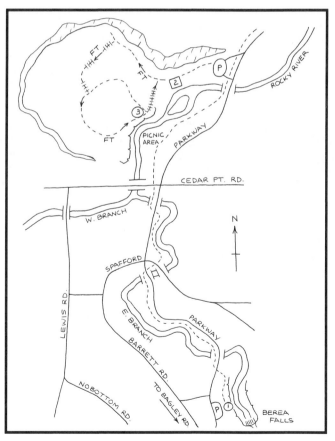

ROCKY RIVER RESERVATION

15 MOHICAN-MEMORIAL STATE FOREST

Distance: Day hikes of 2.4 and 4.6 miles
Terrain: hilly; steep areas

The Mohican-Memorial State Forest offers excellent hiking through the scenic gorge of the Clear Fork River. The latter is a branch of the Mohican River, which itself is a major tributary of the Muskingum. The State Forest covers over 5100 acres, most of which spreads along and southward from the Clear Fork River. Mohican State Park stretches along the west shore of Pleasant Hill Reservoir and through central sections of the gorge.

Designated a National Natural Landmark, the Clear Fork Gorge harbors an extensive beech-hemlock forest. Upper slopes and ridgetops are cloaked by beech-maple and oak-hickory woodlands. Native wildlife includes white-tailed deer, wild turkeys, red squirrels and ruffed grouse. Twenty-one species of warbler summer in the Forest.

Access to the hiking trail network is via a parking lot on the south side of the River, adjacent to the Covered Bridge (CB). The latter structure, completed in 1969, offers your first view of the gorge. Among the many trails that wind through the Mohican-Memorial State Forest, the following routes are suggested for day hikes.

Trail Routes:

Lyons Falls Trail (A). Perhaps the most popular and most scenic hike at Mohican-Memorial State Forest is the Lyons Falls Trail. This 1.6 mile loop can be extended to 2.4 miles by including a side excursion to the base of Little Lyons Falls (2). From the parking lot on Forest Road 8, just south of the Covered Bridge, hike westward into the woods. The trail undulates along the south wall of the gorge, winding through outcrops of sandstone. After hiking approximately ½ miles, turn left onto a rocky trail that leads up to Big Lyons Falls (1). A gentle ascent along the sidestream leads to the base of the falls, which is backed by a recessed cave.

Hike behind the cascade and climb out of this side-gorge via a sandstone stairway. Hike eastward above the ravine and then angle to the north, soon arriving atop Little Lyons Falls (2). Cross the stream above the Falls, ascend the slope and proceed to a trail intersection. Turn right and descend back into the Clear Fork Gorge.

After the trail levels out along the River, watch for a cutoff to the base of Little Lyons Falls, on your right. This short trail leads through a narrow, steep-walled ravine and ends amidst spectacular sandstone formations beneath the Falls. Return to the primary loop, turn right and hike back to the parking area.

Hog Hollow Trail (B). This 2.3 mile trail (4.6 miles roundtrip) also begins at the parking lot on Forest Road 8, just south of the Covered Bridge. Hike eastward, cross a stream and angle to the south. A long, gradual climb parallels the creek (and Forest Road 8) and takes you up the south wall of Clear Fork Gorge. Nearing the top, the trail angles to the east, cuts past the Mohican Youth Center (3) and eventually emerges onto Forest Road 1. Cross the road and climb the Fire Tower (F) which offers a splendid view of the Mohican-Memorial Forest region. Return to the parking area via the same route.

Directions:

From I-71, take Exit #169 (5 miles south of Mansfield) and drive south on S.R. 13 for 5.5 miles. In Bellville, turn east onto S.R. 97 and proceed 11.5 miles to Mohican Memorial State Forest. The entrance to Forest Roads #1 and #8 will be on your left, .8 mile beyond the State Forest sign.

Coming from the east, follow S.R. 3 south from Loudonville. Drive 2 miles and turn right (west) onto S.R. 97. Proceed 2.8 miles to the entrance, on your right.

Little Lyons Falls

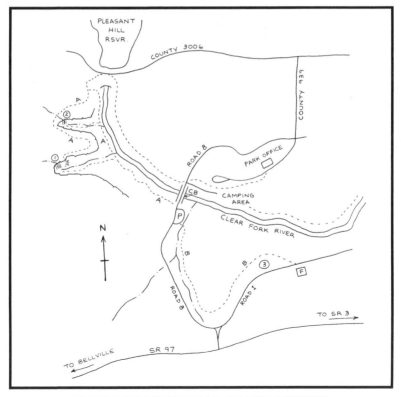

MOHICAN-MEMORIAL STATE FOREST

16 THE WILDERNESS CENTER

Distance: Day hikes of 1.3 and 2.75 miles
Terrain: rolling; some hills with moderate grades

If you seek more than an avenue for exercise .... if the sights, sounds and smells of nature are as important to you as the miles that you log .... consider a visit to the Wilderness Center. Tucked away in the rolling hills of Stark County, the Preserve offers a peaceful retreat from the stress of urban life. Picturesque Amish farms dot the countryside and the noise of human "progress" is far removed.

The Wilderness Center, established in 1964, now encompasses 573 acres, covering an excellent diversity of habitat. Perhaps best known for its parcel of virgin hardwood forest, Sigrist Woods, the Center also harbors an eight-acre lake, a woodland pond, marsh, upland forest, meadows and a re-established prairie. Floodplain woodlands line the course of Fox and Sugar Creeks. An Interpretive Center (1) houses the refuge offices, a gift shop and educational exhibits.

Six trails wind through the Preserve, providing access for hikers and students of nature. The area is popular for cross-country ski tours during the winter months. The following two day hikes are suggested. Please refer to the map in this guide which depicts their routes and the location of parking areas. A more complete but less detailed map is provided by the Center.

Trail Routes:
Pond Trail (A). This 1.3 mile loop begins on the south side of the Interpretive Center (1). Hike westward and bear left, descending through the forest. Bypass a cutoff to the Wilderness Walk and proceed to the Woodland Pond (2). A duck blind sits on the south shore and offers an excellent site for viewing the resident wildlife.

Continue southward to an observation deck (3) that yields a view of the lake basin, framed by towering spruce trees. The trail then descends into the basin, passing along the east shore of the lake. Canada geese and great blue herons will be found here through much of the year and waterfowl may be abundant during migrations. A gazebo (4) juts out from the shore, offering a shady reststop and an convenient lookout for viewing the lake.

Ascending back to the Center, the route cuts through a swath of forest, crosses an open meadow and returns to the main parking lot.

November snow ushers in the quiet season.

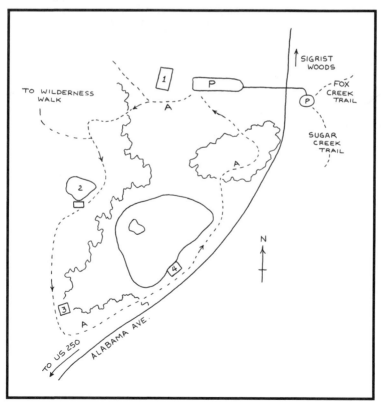

THE POND TRAIL

Sigrist Woods Trail (B) / Pioneer Path (C). This combined hike, yielding a total distance of 2.75 miles, begins at the parking lot for Sigrist Woods. This small lot is on the east side of Alabama Ave., .2 mile north of the Interpretive Center entrance (see map).

Hike northward on the **Sigrist Woods Trail (B)**, crossing Fox Creek and its adjacent wetland via a boardwalk. Reaching higher ground, the trail forks for a loop through Sigrist Woods, a 30 acre parcel of virgin hardwood forest. Bear right onto the loop, passing huge oak, beech, white ash, basswood and black walnut trees. Dogwood, spice bush and maple-leaved viburnum thrive beneath these giants and wildflowers are abundant here in April and May.

Proceed to the northwest end of the loop and angle to the right on a spur trail that leads down to Alabama Ave. Turn right on the road, walk approximately 50 yards and pick up the **Pioneer Path (C)** which begins at a small parking lot. Bear right onto the easternmost segment of the trail, winding through a mixed, immature woodland. You will soon emerge along the southern edge of a large clearing, an area where the Wilderness Center is working to re-establish prairie habitat. Climb gradually along the eastern side of the grassland and, at the top of the slope, pause to enjoy a sweeping view to the south.

Bear right at the trail intersection and enter the woods. The trail dips through a ravine and curves to the east, paralleling the stream to its source at a natural spring (5). Heading back toward the west, the route crosses mature forest and then descends southward, entering a moist, immature woodland.

Exit onto the prairie once again, cross through the trail intersection and hike along the south edge of the field. The trail soon curves to the right and descends through mixed woodland to the parking area. Walk south on Alabama Ave. to the Sigrist Woods lot, completing your hike.

Directions:

From I-77, take Exit #87. Proceed northwest on U.S. 250 for 8 miles to Wilmot. Continue on U.S. 250 through town and drive another mile. Cross Sugar Creek and turn right onto Alabama Ave. The Interpretive Center will be a .6 mile on your left and the Sigrist Woods lot will be .8 mile, on your right.

The Wilderness Center is a nonprofit organization that relies on membership funds and volunteer services to support its conservation efforts. For more information, write to the Center at the address listed in Appendix II.

*Entering
Sigrist Woods*

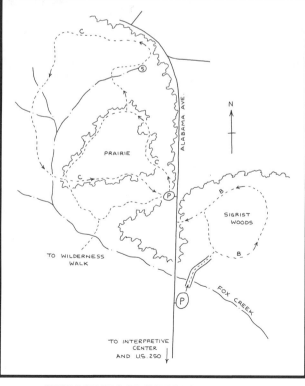

SIGRIST WOODS/PIONEER PATH

17 GAHANNA WOODS STATE NATURE PRESERVE

Distance: 1.5 miles
Terrain: flat/gently rolling

Gahanna Woods State Nature Preserve, just east of Columbus, is a 51 acre refuge characterized by open fields, a beech-maple woodland and embedded areas of swamp forest. Acquired through the efforts of the Nature Conservancy, the Preserve is now managed by the Ohio Department of Natural Resources.

A 1.5 mile hike along Gahanna's trail network will take you through a variety of natural habitats. The following route is suggested.

Trail Route:

From the parking lot, in Gahanna City Park, walk southward and cross the foot-bridge. Angle to the right and follow the **Woodland Pond Trail (WPT)** as it parallels the creek and then winds into the forest. You will soon begin to skirt the edge of a swampland that stretches north-to-south through the drier beech-maple woods. Shallow ponds, buttonbush and moisture-loving trees (pin oak, silver maple, swamp white oak) characterize this boggy area. Skunk cabbage blooms here in early spring as peepers call from the shallows. Wood ducks haunt the larger pools and rotting logs are home to four-toed salamanders.

At the trail intersection, bear left and continue on the **Woodland Pond Trail**.

Hike another .25 mile and turn right along the **Beechwoods Trail (BT)** as it loops through the drier forest. In a few areas, huge beech trees have fallen across the trail and their jumbled remains provide shelter for deer mice, chipmunks and other forest creatures. Pileated woodpeckers are often seen in this area.

Back at the boardwalk intersection, turn right and retrace part of your route along the **Woodland Pond Trail**. Turn left onto the **Beechwoods Trail**, exiting the forest, and wind across the Preserve's open grassland. Red fox and white-tailed deer may be spotted here at dusk. From mid summer to early fall, wildflowers explode across these fields. Milkweed attracts monarch butterflies and stands of prickly ash, clustered along the edge of the forest, provide breeding habitat for giant swallowtails. Gahanna Woods is also home to four rare moth species which depend on its unique combination of habitat.

Directions:

From I-270, east of Columbus, take Exit #39 and proceed east on S.R. 16 for less than .5 mile. Turn left (north) on Taylor Station Road. Drive 2.3 miles to Gahanna City Park, on your left. The Nature Preserve is just south of the park.

Autumn paints the refuge.

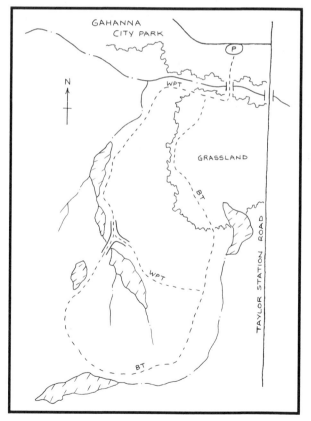

GAHANNA WOODS

18 BLACKHAND GORGE STATE NATURE PRESERVE

Distance: Day hikes of 2.5, 6.5 and 9.0 miles
Terrain: flat along river; hilly side loops

The Licking River, a major tributary of the Muskingum River, has carved a beautiful gorge through the rolling countryside of central Ohio. Natural erosion and human activity have exposed spectacular formations of the Blackhand Conglomerate bedrock, which formed from sea sediments of the Mississippian Period.

The 970 acre Blackhand Gorge State Nature Preserve, dedicated in September, 1975, stretches for 4.5 miles along the Licking River. Access to the Preserve is via an excellent network of trails.

Trail Routes:

The primary hike/bike path, known as the **Blackhand Trail (A)**, follows the abandoned bed of the Central Ohio Railroad. This paved route winds for 4.5 miles along the south bank of the Licking River, offering constant views of this scenic stream. At one point, known as the Deep Cut (1), the trail passes 700 feet through a huge outcropping of the Blackhand Conglomerate. Stands of hemlock cloak north-facing slopes while an oak-hickory forest spreads across the drier, sun-exposed hillsides.

The **Quarry Trail (B)** is a 1.25 mile path that leaves the **Blackhand Trail** approximately ¼ mile west of the parking lot. It first ascends to higher ground and loops past an extensive buttonbush swamp (2). After dipping across the swamp's inlet channel, the trail climbs into the higher, drier forest and skirts the abandoned excavations (3) of past quarry activity. Several overlooks offer views of the remnant rock cliffs, reflected in the still waters of the quarry floor. Near the end of the loop, the trail approaches a modern railroad that crosses the Licking and runs along the northern wall of the gorge. Turn right onto

the **Blackhand Trail** to return to the parking area, completing a 2.5 mile hike.

Approximately .75 mile upstream from the **Quarry Trail** is the entrance to the **Owl Hollow Loop (C)** and **Chestnut Trail (D)**. Both are accessed via a series of stairways that ascend through a scenic ravine. The **Owl Hollow Loop** adds 1 mile to your hike but offers little unique scenery or topography. The **Chestnut Trail**, 2.5 miles in length, angles to the southwest and ascends along the primary stream channel. It then turns northward and climbs higher onto the ridge, crossing through an area of dense, immature forest. Emerging into more open woods, the trail hugs the south wall of Blackhand Gorge and winds westward. Christmas ferns are abundant along the path and mountain laurel clings to the dry, rocky slopes. After crossing several drainages, the trail descends from the ridge and intersects the **Blackhand Trail**. A roundtrip hike along the **Blackhand** and **Chestnut Trails** yields a hike of approximately 6.5 miles.

A combined hike along all four trails . . . **Blackhand, Quarry, Owl Hollow** and **Chestnut** . . . yields a total roundtrip distance of 9.0 miles.

Directions:

To reach Blackhand Gorge State Nature Preserve, follow S.R. 16 east from Newark. Drive approximately 7 miles and exit onto S.R. 146, toward Zanesville. Proceed .1 mile and turn right (south) onto County Road 273, toward Tobosco. Drive 1.7 miles, cross the Licking River and watch for the Preserve's main parking lot, on your right.

Additional trails, not included in this guide, are accessed via the North Parking Lot, on Rockhaven Road (see map).

Entering the "Deep Cut"

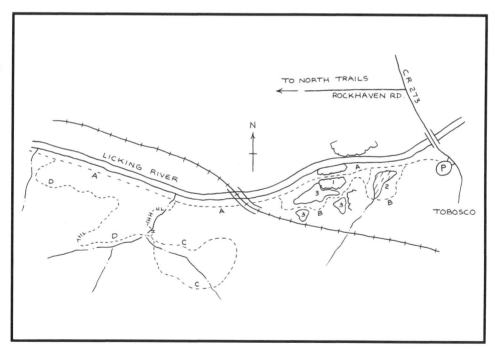

BLACKHAND GORGE STATE NATURE PRESERVE

IV. HIKING AREAS OF NORTHEAST OHIO

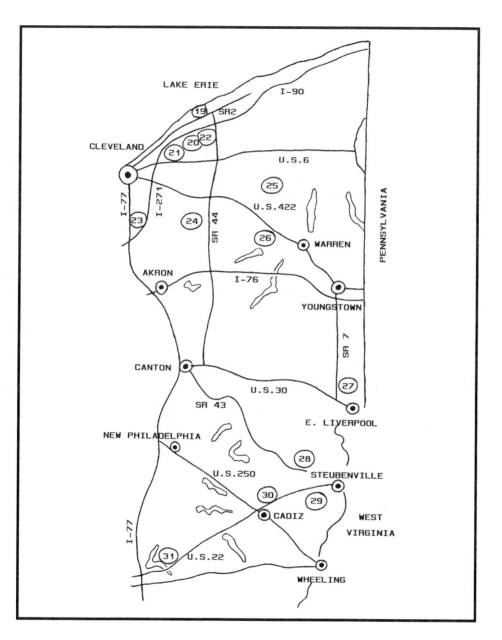

HIKING AREAS OF NORTHEAST OHIO

19 MENTOR MARSH/HEADLAND DUNES

Distance: Day hikes of 4.0 and 6.5 miles
Terrain: rolling

Mentor Marsh State Nature Preserve, dedicated in 1973, protects 619 acres of a salt-marsh grass/cattail wetland that occupies the abandoned channel of the Grand River. Some 500-1000 years ago, the River cut through its northernmost bend, emptying directly into Lake Erie and leaving a 4-mile channel of shallow wetlands along its previous route to the west. With time, the pools and mudflats gave way to open marshlands which, in turn, were invaded by swamp forest. By the mid 20th Century a vast woodland of elm, maple, pin oak and ash covered most of the basin. However, through the 1960s and 1970s, rising water levels and influx of salt from its feeder streams re-converted the wetland to open marsh, now dominated by Phragmites communis, also known as salt-marsh grass or reed grass. Only dead stumps persist where swamp forest once flourished.

The forbidding world of reed grass, which rises twelve feet by mid summer, harbors a vast array of plant and animal life. Pockets of cattail persist throughout the basin and small parcels of swamp forest still cling to its rim. Marsh wrens, bitterns, soras and rails, all more often heard than seen, stalk the dense wetland. Dead timber offers nesting cavities for wood ducks, red-headed woodpeckers, eastern bluebirds and prothonotary warblers. Teal, moorhens and herons may be spotted along the open pools where turtles, frogs and an occasional water snake come to bask in the sun. Resident mammals include beaver, muskrats, mink, weasels, raccoons, red fox and opossums.

A concerted effort to protect the Marsh was initiated in 1960 when plans to "develop" the area were uncovered. Through the efforts of the Ohio Nature Conservancy, the Cleveland Museum of Natural History, the Audubon Society and other conservation organizations, attention was drawn to the unique natural features of the basin. Land donations by the Morton Salt Company and Diamond-Shamrock ensured success of the effort and the Preserve received designation as a National Natural Landmark in 1966.

Trail Route:

A 6.5 mile roundtrip hike takes you along the western rim of Mentor Marsh and out to the Headlands Dunes State Nature Preserve on the shore of Lake Erie. This route corresponds with the northernmost section of the **Buckeye Trail (BT)**.

Park in the lot at the east end of Rosemary Lane (see map). Enter the woods via a spur trail which soon intersects the **Zimmerman Trail (ZT)**, named for a former president of the Burrough Nature Club, a group that was instrumental in the protection of Mentor Marsh. Turn left and hike eastward through the beech-maple-oak forest, crossing numerous drainage channels. Views of the marsh are extensive from late October to early May but maple leaves obscure the vistas during the warmer months. The **Zimmerman/Buckeye Trail** parallels the west shore of the marsh, curving to the north and eventually emerging onto Headlands Drive. Returning to your car at this point yields a roundtrip hike of 4.0 miles.

To continue out to Headlands Dunes, hike eastward along the road. The **Buckeye Trail** cuts through a service area (see map) but I recommend crossing the bridge and proceeding along the road for .5 mile to the State Park entrance. Turn left (north), cut directly through the vast parking lots of the Park and turn right on the paved walk that runs west-east between the lots and the beach. The walkway leads eastward to the Headlands Dunes State Nature

*Mentor Marsh
from the
Zimmerman
Trail*

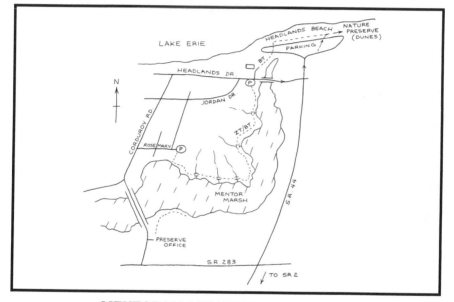

MENTOR MARSH/HEADLANDS AREA

Preserve. Dedicated in 1976, this Preserve protects a small remnant of the once extensive Lake Erie dune habitat, most of which has succumbed to "beach development." Within this sandy refuge are native plants of the Atlantic Coastal Plain, including beach grass, sea rocket and seaside spurge. Switchgrass stabilizes the dunes which are later colonized by wild rye, red osier and sandbar willow. If left undisturbed, cottonwoods and black oaks will eventually invade the area.

After a refreshing stroll along Ohio's North Shore, return to the Mentor Marsh parking area via the same route, completing a roundtrip hike of 6.5 miles.

Directions:

From S.R. 2, east of Cleveland, exit onto S.R. 44 North. Drive .5 mile and exit onto S.R. 273. Turn left (west) and proceed .8 mile to Corduroy Road. Turn right (north) and drive .9 mile, crossing over the marsh, and turn right onto Rosemary Lane. Proceed to the parking lot at the east end of this road.

20 CHAPIN STATE FOREST

Distance: 3.5 miles
Terrain: rolling; steep ascent and descent of ridge

Gildersleeve Mountain is the somewhat overstated title for a low ridge in southern Lake County. Though less than 200 feet higher than its immediate surroundings, the ridge does rise steeply and a few clearings along its northern rim offer broad views that extend to Lake Erie. This rocky prominance is also the centerpiece of Chapin State Forest.

The site of previous quarry activity, the Forest now offers a pleasant retreat for day hikes. Its two trail loops are a walker's delight; wide, even and well-marked, the trails share part of their course with the route of the **Buckeye Trail (BT)**.

Trail Route:

Park in the lot just west of S.R. 306, .9 miles north of U.S. 6. Follow the wide path that leads uphill between the shelter (1) and an old quarry pond (2). This is the first segment of the **Quarry Pond Loop Trail (A)**. The trail curves to the right and winds through a picnic area before leading westward through the forest. After hiking approximately .25 mile, you will notice blue blazes along the path, indicating that you have merged with the **Buckeye Trail**. Curving to the south, you will soon reach another picnic area (3) where the **Quarry Pond Loop**, blazed with red, cuts back to the east.

Continue straight ahead on the **Buckeye Trail**, emerging onto the Forest Road. Turn right and walk along the road for .4 mile to the Ledges Picnic Area (4). Just west of the turn-around loop, the **Buckeye Trail** climbs onto the east flank of Gildersleeve Mountain. As you ascend the slope you will pass outcroppings of Sharon Conglomerate, a resistent Pennsylvanian bedrock that caps the ridge. Bypass the **Ledges Trail (C)** and continue up to the

Lucky Stone Loop (B). This elongated loop winds around the rim of Gildersleeve Mountain, covering a distance of almost 1.5 miles.

Bear right onto the **Lucky Stone Loop** and proceed out to the overlook (5) at the north end of the ridge. Leaves obscure the view in summer but winter visitors are treated to a sweeping panorama of Lake County. Return to the loop and hike along the west rim of the ridge. Clearings above the abandoned quarry site (6) yield broad views to the north, which, on a clear day, extend to Lake Erie.

Bypass the **Wintergreen (D)** and **Mourning Cloak (E) Links** and hike to the southwest end of the ridge where another trail descends to the Chapin Forest Aboretum. Remain on the **Lucky Stone Loop (B)**, curving back to the northeast. Outcroppings of the Sharon Conglomerate are impressive along the east wall of the ridge where fractures and subsequent erosion have created free-standing "stacks." The **Ledges Trail (C)** dips below the rocky shelves while the main loop stays atop the ridge.

After completing the loop, descend from Gildersleeve Mountain and hike back along the Forest Road to the **Quarry Pond Loop (A)**. The south arm of this loop is currently under construction and, if not completed, you may wish to return to your car via the road or retrace your initial route along the north arm.

Directions:

From U.S. 6 east of Greater Cleveland, turn north on S.R. 306. Drive .9 mile and turn left (west) into Chapin State Forest (this entrance is approximately 2 miles south of Kirtland). Park in the first lot on your right, just west of S.R. 306.

A pause on the trail

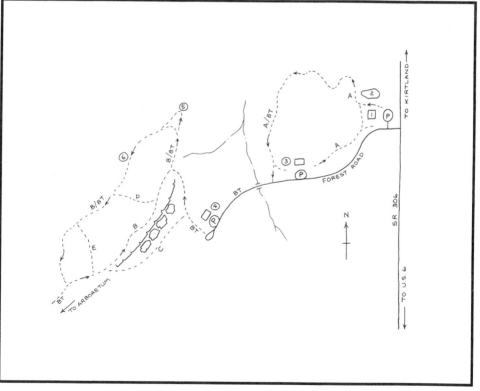

CHAPIN STATE FOREST

21 HACH-OTIS SANCTUARY STATE NATURE PRESERVE

Distance: 1.5 miles
Terrain: rolling; one stairway

Perched atop the west wall of the Chagrin River Valley, Hach-Otis Sanctuary was originally donated to the Cleveland Bird Club in 1944. The 81 acre forest was dedicated as a State Nature Preserve in 1977, protecting its rich bounty of flora and wildlife. Stands of eastern hemlock rise along its deep, shaded ravines while a mixed forest of beech, maple, oak, hickory and tulip poplar cloaks most of the Preserve. Wildflowers, including rare species such as red trillium and pink moccasin flower, are abundant here in April and May. Pileated woodpeckers, barred owls, red squirrels and red efts are among the many wild inhabitants of Hach-Otis Sanctuary.

Trail Route:

Access to the Preserve is provided by a double-loop trail. From the parking area, proceed eastward on the central boardwalk and turn left onto the **North Trail (N)**. Curving to the east the trail skirts a deep ravine and arrives at an overlook of the Chagrin River Valley. Steep walls of shale and glacial till rise above the stream. Continued erosion along these cliffs will gradually widen the valley and eventually claim the hilltop forest. For now, these perilous cliffs offer prime nesting habitat for bank swallows and belted kingfishers.

Proceed southward along the **North Trail**, passing a second overlook (see map) and then cutting into the forest along a drainage channel. Arriving back at the central boardwalk, continue straight ahead and then turn left onto the **South Trail (S)** loop. Nearing the cliffs again, a short spur path leads out to another overlook of the Chagrin Valley. The main loop leads southward, winding above the bluffs and then curves westward along a deep, hemlock-lined ravine. Bypass the short-cut trail (see map) and continue upstream, soon angling back to the north. Descend a wooden stairway, cross the stream and climb onto the next slope, returning to the central boardwalk. Turn left for a short walk to the parking lot.

Directions:

From I-90, east of Cleveland, take Exit #189 and drive south on S.R. 91. Proceed 1 mile and turn left (east) on U.S. 6. Drive 1.2 miles and turn left (north) on S.R. 174. Proceed .1 mile and turn right on Skyline Drive; the parking lot is at the east end of this road.

The Chagrin River Valley

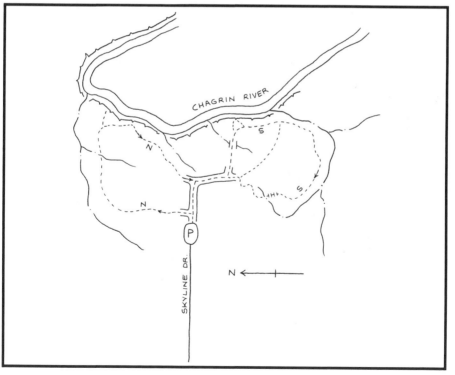

THE HACH-OTIS SANCTUARY

22 HOLDEN ARBORETUM

Distance: 3.2 miles
Terrain: hilly; stairways

Any guide to the natural areas of Ohio would be incomplete without acknowledging the Holden Arboretum. Though an entrance fee is charged, the Arboretum plays a vital role in plant research, habitat conservation and public education. Indeed, this nonprofit Foundation is the Midwest/ Great Lakes headquarters of the Center for Plant Conservation.

Holden Arboretum, encompassing 2900 acres, is the largest arboretum in the United States. While most visitors concentrate within its vast gardens of flowering plants, the Center's natural areas have received designation as a National Natural Landmark. The following 3.2 mile hike takes you away from the crowds and into the post-glacial valley of Pierson's Creek.

Trail Route:

From the south side of the Corning Building (1) and Thayer Center (2), curve westward around a picnic area and descend the stairway behind the shelter house (3). Cross a bridge and turn right, climbing steadily above the west shore of Foster Pond (4).

Bear left at the intersection, walk a short distance and turn right onto the **Old Valley Trail (A)**. This route is blazed with yellow paint and with an odd marker that resembles a "square root" symbol. Descend through the hardwood forest along a stream bed, cross another drainage channel and then negotiate a long stairway, dropping into the Pierson Creek Valley. I thought this might be the longest flight of wooden stairs in Ohio . . . . until I found a matching set further along the trail.

Cross the primary Creek, ascend past a scenic ravine (5) and climb onto the valley wall via a broad switchback. Leveling off for a short distance the trail dips across

another stream before ascending to higher ground. Bypass two cutoff trails that lead to short side-loops (see map).

Curving back to the northeast, the path descends into the Pierson Creek Valley for a second time, crosses the stream and reaches a boardwalk (6) that provides a short tour of this moist, creek-side habitat. Ferns, clubmoss, scouring rush and numerous wildflowers thrive in this sheltered cove of the valley floor. The Arboretum provides a brochure and checklist for plants found in this area.

Climb out of the valley via another long flight of stairs and turn right along the **Woodland Trail (B)**. Walk a short distance and bear right onto another section of the **Old Valley Trail (A)**, winding above a deep side ravine of Pierson's Creek. Merge with the **Woodland Trail** again and hike northward along the edge of Buttonbush Bog (7). Arriving at the south end of Blueberry Pond (8), turn left and hike along the shore of this scenic lake. Conifers along its northern rim give the Pond a true North Woods flavor.

Wind back to the Corning Center, completing a loop hike of approximately 3.2 miles.

Directions:

Take Exit #193 from I-90 and drive south on S.R. 306 toward Kirtland. Proceed 1 mile and turn left (east) on S.R. 615. At the stopsign, proceed straight ahead on Kirtland-Chardon Road. Drive almost 4 miles and turn left (north) on Sperry Road. The Arboretum entrance will be 1.2 miles on your left.

Holden Arboretum is open to visitors Tuesday through Sunday, 10 a.m. to 5 p.m. The admission charge is currently $2.50 per adult and $1.75 for children. For more information, contact the Aboretum via the address or phone number listed in Appendix II.

Blueberry Pond

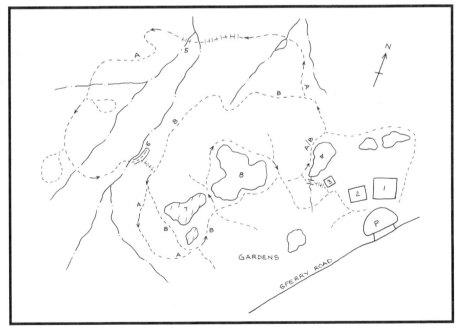

HOLDEN ARBORETUM

Distance: Day hikes of 3.0, 3.4, 3.5, 4.0 and 5.0 miles
Terrain: flat/rolling along Pinery Narrows and Tinkers Gorge trails;
hilly at Ledges and Blue Hen Falls

The Akron-Cleveland area, traditionally depicted as Ohio's industrial corridor, possesses what may be our State's greatest concentration of parks and natural areas. Cleveland's "Emerald Necklace" of parks overlaps with Akron's excellent Metropark system and numerous nature preserves are scattered through the region. The 33,000 acre Cuyahoga Valley National Recreation Area, established in 1974, is the centerpiece of this open-space network and offers numerous hiking opportunities.

Formed after the retreat of the Wisconsin Glacier, some 14,000 years ago, the Valley now channels the Cuyahoga River. Continued erosion along its walls has exposed bedrock spanning 60 million years of geologic history. Deep within the gorge, Chagrin shale, formed from Devonian sea deposits, rises along the banks of the river. Mississippian Period bedrock, including Berea sandstone and Cuyahoga shales, jut from middle segments of the Valley wall. Atop the ridges, Sharon Conglomerate, formed from Pennsylvanian sediments, has eroded into spectacular ledges and recessed caves.

Complete coverage of the Cuyahoga Valley's many geologic, topographic and vegetative features are beyond the scope of this guide. However, the following hikes provide an overview of this vast preserve.

Trail Routes:

Haskel Run/Ledges Area (3.5 mile hike). Park in the Happy Days Visitor Center lot on the north side of S.R. 303, two miles east of Peninsula. Walk to the south, crossing under the road via a tunnel, and continue along the entry road to the Visitor Center (VC). Pick up the **Haskel Run**

Trail (A) as it leads eastward atop a ravine, passing Mater Dolorosa Cemetery (circa 1869), on your left. Wind into the ravine, cross Haskel Run and bear left onto a connector trail to the Ledges Area, part of Virginia Kendall Park.

A short climb brings you to the **Ledges Trail (B)**, which makes a 2.5 mile loop around a plateau of Sharon Conglomerate. This Pennsylvanian bedrock is composed primarily of sandstone and quartz arenite and overlies Meadville Shale of the late Mississippian Period. Water erosion has carved spectacular ledges, recessed caves and "balanced rock" formations from the rugged walls of the plateau.

Turn right onto the **Ledges Trail** loop and hike southward, bypassing several cutoffs to the Ledges and Octagon shelters. Red squirrels chatter from the numerous hemlocks and chipmunks scamper among the rock crevices. At the sound end of the loop, wind up to the Overlook which provides a broad view of the Cuyahoga Valley.

After taking in the vista, hike eastward along the south edge of the plateau's central field. Cross the Ledges entry road and begin a gradual descent through the forest. A wooden bridge takes you across a side ravine and the rock ledges soon reappear above the trail. Another .25 mile brings you to "Ice Box Cave (C)," a squared recess in the rock wall. Continue to the north end of the **Ledges Trail** loop and descend back to Haskel Run. Turn left on the **Haskel Run Trail (A)**, re-cross the creek and climb steeply to the top of the ridge. You will emerge onto a large field that extends west from the Visitor Center. Cross the field and return to the parking lot.

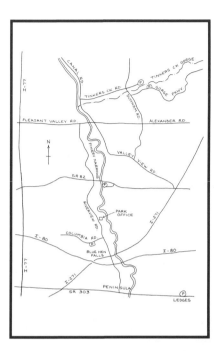

The Ledges Overlook

CUYAHOGA VALLEY
NATIONAL RECREATION AREA

HASKEL RUN
AND
LEDGES TRAILS

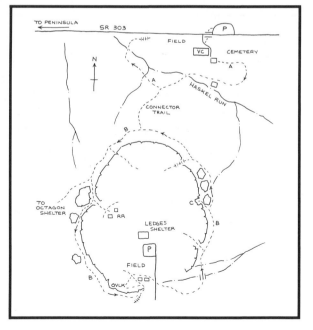

Blue Hen Falls/Columbia Run Gorge (3.4 miles roundtrip). Park in the small, graveled pull-off on the south side of Columbia Road, .5 mile west of Riverview Road (this is .3 mile east of where the **Buckeye Trail** crosses Columbia Road). Hike southward, intersecting the **Buckeye Trail (BT)**, blazed with blue paint. Bear left and wind into the Columbia Run Gorge where hemlocks thrive in the cool, moist ravines. Cross the stream and ascend along a deep ravine that cuts southward from Columbia Run. Once atop the slope you begin a long hike along the crest of the ridge.

After hiking almost 1 mile across the flat ridgetop, you will cross a power line swath and descend into the next valley. At the bottom of the slope a side trail leads off to the left, ending at an overlook of Blue Hen Falls. Enjoy a picnic lunch above this scenic cascade and then return to your car via the same route.

Pinery Narrows (5 miles roundtrip). This hike takes you along the abandoned towpath of the Ohio and Erie Canal, paralleling a secluded section of the Cuyahoga River. Park in the graveled clearing below the S.R. 82 bridge, on the east bank of the river (see Directions). Hike northward through the Valley with the Canal on your right and the Cuyahoga River on your left.

Water flow is maintained through this section of the Canal, attracting Canada geese, wood ducks, herons and kingfishers. Wildflowers are abundant across the floodplain and waterfalls spring from the shale cliffs from March to June. Sycamores and maples tower above the river banks, the latter providing a colorful display in October. Upon reaching Canal Road, turn around and retrace your hike through the Valley.

The Cuyahoga River in Pinery Narrows

Blue Hen Falls

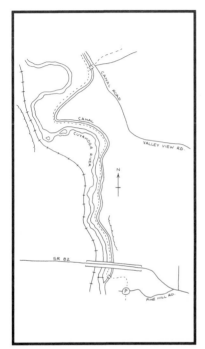

THE PINERY NARROWS

**TRAIL TO
BLUE HEN FALLS**

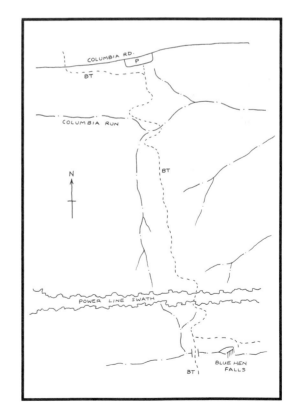

Tinkers Creek Gorge (hikes of 3.0 and 4.0 miles). Two trail routes offer different perspectives on the rugged gorge of Tinkers Creek.

The **Gorge Trail (A).** Park in the lot at the east end of Tinkers Creek Road and pick up the trail at the northeast corner of the baseball field (beyond the left field corner). Enter the woodland and bear right at the fork in the trail, winding along the rocky stream. Cleveland Shale, of late Devonian age, is exposed in the lower recesses of the gorge. As you hike eastward and upward you will travel forward in geologic time, passing through Bedford shale and Berea Sandstone of the Mississippian Period. Hemlocks cluster along the shaded, north-facing slopes while oak forest predominates across the dry, thin soils of the gorge. Stream crossings can pose a problem during high water season and the distance of your hike will vary accordingly. The maximum roundtrip hike through the Gorge will be approximately 4 miles.

Buckeye Trail/Gorge Parkway. A section of the **Buckeye Trail (BT)** winds across the south rim of Tinkers Creek Gorge; most of its route is in close proximity to the Gorge Parkway and the paved bike path (BP). Park at the Gorge Overlook lot, on the Gorge Parkway, just east of the intersection with Overlook Lane. The Overlook itself is a National Natural Landmark and yields a breathtaking view of Tinkers Creek Gorge.

Hike eastward along the road and watch for the **Buckeye Trail** as it crosses west to east. Angle to the left and continue eastward along the trail, beginning a 1.5 mile excursion across the south rim of the gorge. You will soon reach Bridal Veil Falls (F) and then ascend to the Lonesome Meadow Picnic Area (LMP). At the next road crossing, turn left for a short walk to another overlook of Tinkers Creek Gorge. Using this scenic spot as your endpoint, return to your car via the same route, completing a roundtrip hike of 3.0 miles.

Directions:

To reach the Happy Days Visitor Center and the Haskels Run/Ledges Trail, take Exit 12 from I-271 and drive east on S.R. 303. The lot will be 4.7 miles, on the north side of the road.

To reach the access point for the hike to Blue Hen Falls, take Exit 12 from I-271 and drive east on S.R. 303 for 2 miles, into the town of Peninsula. Turn left (north) on Riverview Road and drive 2.6 miles. Turn left on Columbia Road and proceed .5 mile to the graveled pull-off, on your left.

The south access for the Pinery Narrows is reached via Pine Hill Road which cuts back to the west from S.R. 82, just east of the Cuyahoga River bridge. Take Exit 149A from I-77 and drive east on S.R. 82 for 4.1 miles to this cutoff. Descend a gravel road to the River's floodplain.

To reach Tinkers Creek Gorge, take the Independence Exit from I-77 and drive east on Pleasant Valley Road. Cross the River and turn left (north) on Canal Road. Proceed almost 1 mile and turn right on Tinkers Creek Road. Drive 1.8 miles to the Dunham Road crossing and proceed to parking areas as illustrated on the map.

The rocky bed of Tinkers Creek

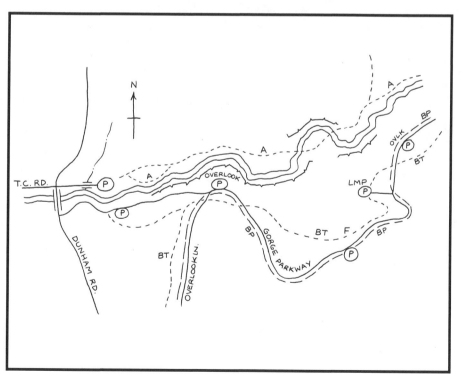

TINKERS CREEK GORGE

24 TINKERS CREEK STATE NATURE PRESERVE

Distance: 2.75 miles
Terrain: flat

For those enamored by wetlands, a visit to Tinkers Creek State Nature Preserve is a must. This 786 acre refuge, in the upper watershed of Tinkers Creek, is part of a vast, watery oasis. The area is characterized by freshwater ponds, mixed woodlands and an extensive, open marsh. This natural wetland was actually expanded by man's handiwork; the construction of a railroad embankment along the western edge of the swamp impaired flow through Tinkers Creek and spread marshy shallows across the flatlands to the east.

As is true with most wetlands, wildlife is abundant at Tinkers Creek. Canada geese, wood ducks and great blue herons will be found here throughout the year while migrant waterfowl peak in March and November. Other migrants include osprey, rails, and bitterns. Beaver, muskrats, red fox, white-tailed deer, raccoons and mink are among the resident mammals. Watch for frogs, water snakes, four-toed salamanders and snapping turtles along the ponds. Insects can be bothersome in summer and use of a repellent is strongly advised.

Trail Route:
From the parking lot, cross Old Mill Road and hike southward along the entry trail. White pines tower above the trail which soon intersects the **Seven Ponds Trail (A)**. Continue straight ahead on this 1.75 mile loop, skirting the western shore of two ponds and crossing to the east side of a

third. At the south end of the loop, turn right onto the **South Point Trail (B)**. This path runs atop a finger of relatively high ground, cloaked by an oak woodland, that extends out into the open marsh. From its course one can easily peruse the surrounding swamplands.

Return to the **Seven Ponds Trail** and bear right. An observation platform (0), reached by a short spur trail, provides a sweeping view of the Tinkers Creek marsh. The main trail continues northward, winding past several ponds and crossing boggy ground via raised boardwalks.

Angle to the right on the **Lonesome Pond Trail (C)** for a .5 mile excursion around the northernmost pond. Beavers have colonized this spring-fed lake and signs of their activity will be noted along the trail. Returning to the **Seven Ponds Trail** turn right, completing the loop and follow the entry trail to the parking lot.

Directions:
From the Greater Cleveland area, follow I-480 toward the southeast. Take Exit #41 (Frost Road), proceed to the east side of the highway and turn left (north) on a road across from the Sohio station. Drive .4 mile to the stopsign and turn left on a street that becomes Ravenna Road. Proceed 2.2 miles and turn right (east) on Old Mill Road. The Preserve's parking lot will be .8 mile on your left, just across the railroad tracks.

One of seven ponds along the trail

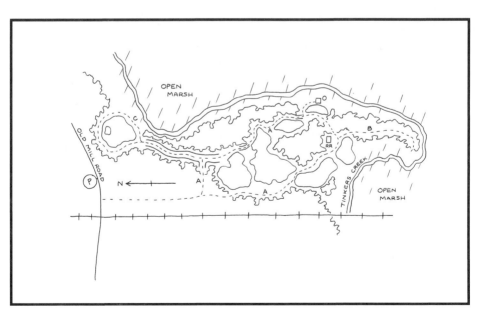

THE TINKERS CREEK PRESERVE

25 SWINE CREEK RESERVATION

Distance: 3.0 miles
Terrain: hilly; few steep areas; one stairway

Established in 1981, Swine Creek Reservation became the fourth Park in the Geauga County Park District. The Preserve's 331 acres are draped across a series of forested ravines southeast of Middlefield, Ohio. An excellent network of trails provides access to the Park's varied terrain and these well-marked paths are popular for cross-country skiing during the winter months. A lodge (1) serves as an educational center throughout the year and offers a warm retreat on cold winter days.

Trail Route:

The following 3-mile hike uses sections of the Park's six interconnecting trails and crosses through its many habitats.

Enter the Park off Hayes Road and bear left toward the Lodge (1). Park across from the Lodge and cross the pond via a bridge. Turn north along a wide path; this is the initial segment of the **Gray Fox (GF)** and **Squaw Root (SR) Trails**. Curving to the left, the trail forks; bear right onto the **Gray Fox Trail** and descend along the edge of a meadow. My wife and I spotted a red fox and her cubs here on a late May afternoon. Bypass the cutoff on your left, climb northward and bear left at the next fork, cutting into the forest. Cross over the **Siltstone Trail (ST)** and you will soon emerge along the Park road.

Loop back to the left and continue on the **Gray Fox Trail**, crossing a small stream. The trail angles to the west, crosses another drainage channel and intersects the **Wagon Trail (WT)**. This wide, graveled path is used for hayrides in the summer and sleigh rides in the winter. Turn right on the **Wagon Trail**, walk a short distance and cross a paved loop that services the Sugar House (2) where maple syrup is distilled in early spring.

Proceed northward along the **Gray Fox Trail** which cuts behind a shelter house (3). Watch for skier plaques overhead on the trees since this section of the trail is indistinct. Winding to the northwest the path leaves the forest and follows the edge of an open field. It then loops back to the south and crosses another meadow. Watch for white-tailed deer in these clearings at dawn or dusk. Re-entering the forest the trail begins a long excursion through the beech-maple-oak woodland, winding above a deep gorge to the west.

Curving back to the north, cross an abandoned road and a side stream and then turn right onto the **Glen Trail (GT)** which descends into a ravine. Ascend the opposite slope via a long stairway and turn right on the **Wagon Trail**. Follow this graveled loop to its southern end and angle right onto the **Valley Trail (VT)** which cuts in next to a bench.

Begin a long, gradual descent into the Swine Creek Valley and, along the way, bypass two narrow paths on your right. Cross the creek and head upstream along the valley floor, re-crossing the braided channel at several points. After walking about .3 mile upstream, watch for a cutoff trail **(CT)** on your right that ascends the east wall of the valley. Climb along this trail and you will soon intersect the **Gray Fox Trail**. Turn right, ascend along the field and return to the Lodge area.

Directions:

From Middlefield, Ohio, drive south on S.R. 608, cross over S.R. 528 and turn left (east) on Swine Creek Road. Proceed 2 miles and turn left (north) on Hayes Road. Drive .5 mile to the Park entrance, on your left. Enter the Preserve and bear left toward the Lodge area.

The Swine Creek Lodge

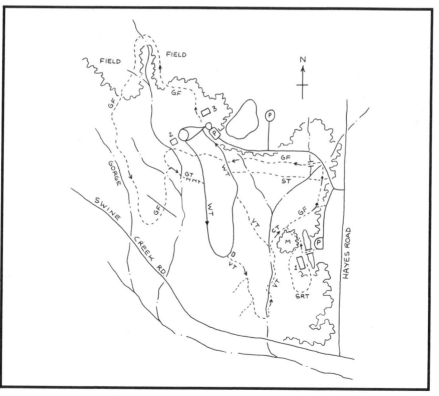

SWINE CREEK RESERVATION

26 EAGLE CREEK STATE NATURE PRESERVE

Distance: 5.0 miles
Terrain: rolling

Eagle Creek and its many tributaries have eroded a shallow basin across northeastern Portage County. Disrupted by the work of beavers, the stream flows through a vast network of ponds, buttonbush swamps and open marsh. Sphagnum bogs, relics from the Pleistocene Epoch, dot the periphery of the basin and swamp forest spreads along the soggy floodplain.

Dedicated in 1974, Eagle Creek State Nature Preserve protects 440 acres of this rich wetland. The refuge harbors many rare and threatened species, including cucumber magnolia, yellow birch, ostrich ferns, four-toed salamanders and spotted turtles. A 5-mile, double-loop trail provides access to the Preserve.

Trail Route:

From the parking lot along Hopkins Road, hike westward across an open grassland. Bypass a cutoff on your left and enter the forest. Crossing a small drainage channel you will soon arrive at a trail intersection.

Turn right along the **Clubmoss Trail (A)** which snakes northward above the Eagle Creek basin. Skirting a bog, the trail ascends to higher ground and splits into a loop. Bear left on the loop and you will soon reach a spur trail that leads down to an observation blind (1). Before you is a large beaver pond where migrant waterfowl congregate in spring and fall. Canada geese nest along the marshy shores and great blue herons stalk the shallows.

Return to the loop, turn left and continue to the north through the moist, beech-maple forest. Curving to the east, the trail skirts a pond and emerges into an open woodland where wild roses grow in abundance. White-tailed deer and red fox may be spotted here at dawn or dusk. Hawks patrol the meadows by day while great

horned and barred owls emerge from the woods to work the night shift.

Re-enter the forest, soon winding along the edge of a sphagnum bog (2). A boardwalk leads into the bog, permitting close study of its unique flora. Look for glacial relics such as winterberry holly and cottonsedge and for carnivorous sundew and pitcher plants.

Completing the **Clubmoss Trail** loop, turn left (south) and return to the entry area. Proceed southward on the **Beaver Run Trail (B)**, crossing a bridge and soon arriving at a clearing on the edge of the Eagle Creek marshlands. Climbing to higher ground, the trail undulates along the east wall of the basin and eventually descends to the floodplain.

Waterproof boots come in handy as the trail meanders across the flat, soggy ground, crossing sidestreams and passing shallow drainage ponds. After a .5 mile trek across the swampy woodlands you will reach Eagle Creek, spanned by a fine, wooden bridge. Cross the creek and turn northward along its west bank.

Curving westward and ascending above the wetland, the path intersects the **Beech Ridge Trail (C)**. This trail loops through the forest, circling a natural drainage basin, and returns to the **Beaver Run Trail (B)**. Re-cross the floodplain and return to the entry area. Turn right and return to the parking lot, completing a total hike of approximately 5 miles.

Directions:

From S.R. 88 in Garrettsville, turn east on S.R. 82, proceed 2 blocks and turn left (north) on Center Road. Drive northeast on this road for 2.3 miles and turn right (south) on Hopkins Road. The parking lot will be .8 mile, on your right.

The Eagle Creek wetlands harbor many threatened species.

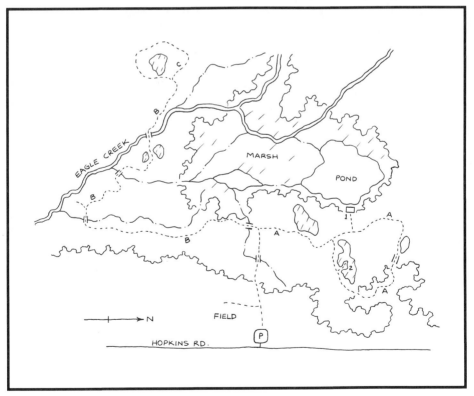

EAGLE CREEK NATURE PRESERVE

27 BEAVER CREEK STATE PARK

Distance: Day hikes of 1.6, 2.5 and 7 miles
Terrain: hilly along Dogwood Trail; flat along stream

One of Ohio's most beautiful streams, Little Beaver Creek was the first inductee into our State's Wild and Scenic River System. Clear, sparkling water, sandstone cliffs, stands of hemlock and a rich, hardwood forest make the area a superb retreat for the naturalist. Beaver Creek State Park, established in 1945, covers over 3000 acres and stretches for seven miles along the valley of Little Beaver Creek.

In addition to its natural beauty, the valley harbors remnants of Ohio's preindustrial era. Hoping to profit from transportation needs during the mid 1800s, a group of businessmen built the Sandy and Beaver Canal along the course of Little Beaver Creek. In its heyday the Canal spawned the growth of several communities in the valley, including Sprucevale, centered near the Hambleton grist mill (2). Stretching for 21 miles from Elkton to East Liverpool, the Canal was abandoned as railroads invaded the State. Crumbled remains of its numerous locks persist along the river today. Old mill buildings dot the valley, one of which, Gaston's Mill (1; circa 1830), has been restored for the education and enjoyment of visitors to the State Park.

Sixteen miles of hiking trails and an equal network of bridal paths provide access to remote areas of the Park. The following day hikes are suggested.

Trail Routes:
Dogwood Trail (A). This 2.5 mile loop begins and ends at Picnic Area #3, on the north side of the Creek and just west of the Park Office/Gaston's Mill area (see map). From the west end of the picnic grounds, angle to the northwest and climb steeply along a white-blazed trail. This hillside is carpeted with white trillium in mid spring. The trail levels out along a rocky terrace and crosses through stands of hemlock. Red squirrels scamper among these conifers, noisily scolding as you approach their favorite tree.

Winding to the north the path loops above a ravine. Bear left at the trail intersection, bypassing a cutoff to the family campgrounds. Views of Little Beaver Creek unfold as you swing back to the southwest. Descending along another sidestream, the route crosses open forest where wildflowers abound in April and May.

At the base of the slope the trail angles to the southwest and skirts the floodplain of Little Beaver Creek. The moist woodlands that line the stream are prime habitat for flycatchers, warblers and tree frogs. Upon reaching the Creek, the **Dogwood Trail** turns back to the east and parallels the stream to Picnic Area #3. Pine woodlands thrive along the north bank while hemlocks cluster on the shaded, north-facing slopes. Rocky cliffs rise above the stream and towering sycamores anchor along its sandy shores. Watch for soft-shelled trutles that sun themselves on the riverbanks, sliding into the water as you approach.

April along Little Beaver Creek

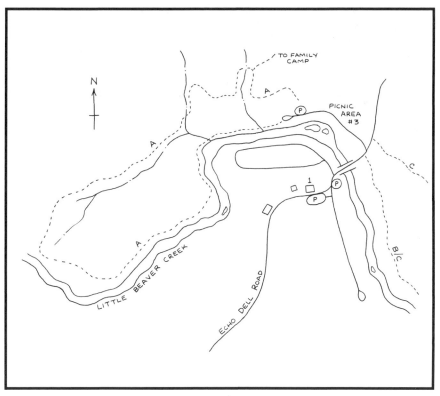

THE DOGWOOD TRAIL

Sandy Beaver Trail (B). This 21 mile trail, maintained by regional Boy Scout troops, follows the abandoned course of the Sandy and Beaver Canal. A 3.5 mile section of the trail winds through Beaver Creek State Park, paralleling the north bank of the river. Six weathered locks are spaced along this portion of the trail, adding historical interest to the spectacular natural scenery. Kingfishers patrol the stream and small flocks of waterfowl (primarily wood ducks and teal) huddle along the shallows. Cliffs of sandstone and shale tower above the creek and giant slump blocks, having broken from the cliffs, rest along the valley floor.

This 3.5 mile section of the **Sandy Beaver Trail** coincides with parts of the State Park Trail network. Specifically, the south arm of the **Vondergreen Trail (C)** is used at the west end and the .8 mile **Gretchen's Lock Trail (D)** near the east end. The trail is accessed by parking areas at Gaston's Mill (1) or at the Group Campgrounds (3), at the former site of Sprucevale.

A complete roundtrip hike between these two access points yields a total distance of 7.0 miles. A shorter alternative is to hike to the remains of Gretchen's Lock (4), .8 mile from the Group Campground (1.6 miles roundtrip). This lock was named for the daughter of E. H. Gill, an engineer who worked on the Canal system. Gretchen died from malaria and was temporarily entombed within the lock until her father returned to Europe.

Directions:
Exit onto S.R. 7 from S.R. 30, just west of East Liverpool, Ohio. Drive north on S.R. 7 for 2 miles and turn right (east) on Bell School Road. Drive 1.1 mile and turn left (north) on Echo Dell Road to reach the Park Office/Gaston's Mill/Dogwood Trail area.

To reach the Group Campground in old Sprucevale, bypass Echo Dell Road and continue eastward on Bell School Road. Drive another 1.5 miles and turn left on Cannon's Mill Road (unmarked). Merge with County Road 428 and proceed north into the valley of Little Beaver Creek. Sprucevale Lookout (5), perched above the abandoned community, offers a spectacular view of the stream and its steep-walled gorge. The Group Campground entrance will be on your left, north of the creek and across the road from Hambleton's Mill (2).

View from Sprucevale Lookout

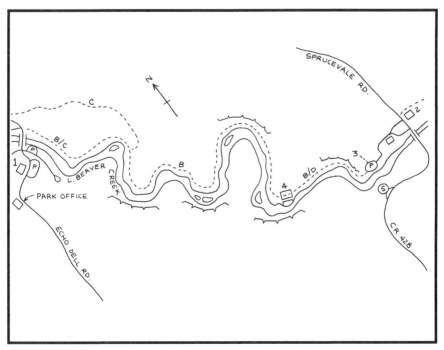

THE SANDY BEAVER TRAIL

28 JEFFERSON LAKE STATE PARK

Distance: Day hikes of 2.5, 3.6 and 4.0 miles
Terrain: rolling along lakeshore; hilly on North Loop

Nestled within the forested hills of Jefferson County, the 933 acres of Jefferson Lake State Park provide a scenic retreat for the residents of eastern Ohio. The Park's 27 acre lake was created by a dam across the Town Fork of Yellow Creek, a project of the Civilian Conservation Corps.

A fifteen-mile network of hiking trails provides access to remote sections of the Park; a restructuring of the network is currently underway and reference to the map in this guide is suggested. The best day hikes originate near the lake and yield distances of 2.5 to 4.0 miles. The following routes are recommended.

Trail Routes:

North Loop (A; my terminology). This 2.5 mile loop begins and ends at the Beach Area on the north shore of Jefferson Lake. Park in the large lot near the Beach (see map) and walk westward along the shore to the Beach Area, crossing an inlet stream. Turn right and walk to the north end of the picnic/playground. Enter the forest on a wide path that parallels the stream and soon crosses it. Ascending gradually to the north, the trail passes an old stone cabin (C) and then curves back to the left, climbing steeply onto the ridge.

At the crest of the hill you will emerge behind the Park Office and Maintenance Center. Turn left for a short distance and then cut westward to the Campground Road (see map). Turn right on this lane, walk about 25 yards and pick up the trail again, just across from Campsite #16 (a sign indicates "to Lake").

Leading west and then south, the trail begins a long descent to the Town Fork of Yellow Creek. Entering the floodplain the trail curves to the left, crosses a sidestream and ascends onto the hillside. It then levels out along a terrace before descending toward the creek again via a switchback. Angling to the east, the path parallels the stream which soon flows through a broad marsh and empties into Jefferson Lake. This backwater wetland is an excellent spot to observe the varied wildlife that inhabits the Park. Continue eastward along the north shore of the lake and return to the Beach Area.

Lakeside Trail (B). Park in the lot along County Road 54, just below the Dam. Cross the footbridge beneath the spillway and follow the trail as it winds along the south shore of Jefferson Lake. A 1.8 mile hike brings you to backwater stream crossings where seasonal flooding and indistinct trails can pose a problem. If you are unable to wind through to the north shore, return to your car via the same route, completing a 3.6 mile hike.

Should you manage to cross the Town Fork, pick up the **North Loop Trail (A)** and turn right, heading east to the Beach Area as described above. Continuing around the lake to the Dam, using County Road #54, your completed loop will total approximately 4.0 miles.

Directions:

From Richmond, Ohio, drive west on S.R. 43. Proceed 1.0 mile and turn right (north) on County Road 54. The Park entrance will be approximately 1.7 miles. Refer to the map for location of parking areas.

View from the north shore

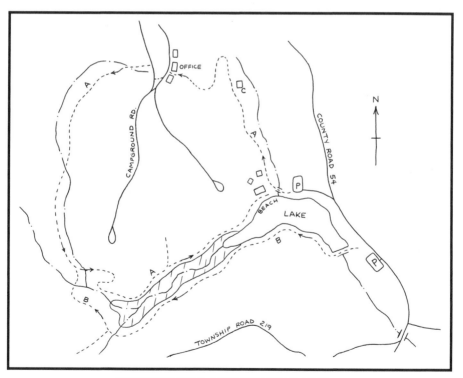

JEFFERSON LAKE STATE PARK

29 FERNWOOD STATE FOREST

Distance: Day hikes of 3.0 and 4.0 miles
Terrain: hilly; moderate grades

Admired by naturalists and despised by loggers, the beaver is second only to man in his impact on the natural environment. Driven by instinct to insure his own survival, the beaver constructs dams that turn sparkling, woodland streams into series of ponds and marshlands. While the new habitats also benefit many other species, the altered drainage often disrupts the lives of local humans.

Fernwood State Forest, four miles south of Wintersville, is an excellent area to witness the impact of these industrious rodents. The preserve is part of the Jefferson Reclamation Area, dedicated in 1969, where reforestation of strip-mined lands was undertaken. The largest segment of the Forest, stretching south from the Cross Creek Valley, is accessed by the Douglas Applegate Road (Township Road 181) and by two trails. The combination of these three avenues yields a loop hike of approximately 4.0 miles.

Trail Route:

From the parking lot for the **Deer Run Trail (A)**, along Douglas Applegate (see map), hike southward into the forest. After a short climb the route begins a long descent into the next valley. The **Deer Run Trail** parallels a drainage channel which, thanks to the beaver, has become a long series of ponds and boggy woodlands. Rugged cliffs of limestone and shale, left behind by previous mining activity, rise above the waterway. Watch for groundhogs that den along these dry, rocky slopes. Chipmunks are abundant in the forest, wary of broad-winged hawks and great horned owls that patrol this remote woodland.

Bypass the few side trails that lead off to the left, remaining on the wide path that parallels the drainage channel. At the bottom of the slope the **Deer Run Trail** crosses a creek and intersects the **Beaver Dam Trail (B)**. This entire area is subject to seasonal flooding, prompted by the handiwork of local beavers. If impassable, return to your car via the same route, completing a hike of 3.0 miles.

If the terrain and your footwear permit, turn right on the **Beaver Dam Trail** and follow this path as it winds upstream, passing a chain of ponds and marshes. The beavers themselves are primarily nocturnal and are best observed at dusk. Gnawed trunks along the trail attest to their active nightlife.

A gradual 1.5 mile climb through the valley brings you to County Road #26. Turn right for a short distance and then turn right onto Douglas Applegate Road. Hike eastward along this scenic drive for .9 mile, returning to the parking lot at the **Deer Run** trailhead. Several vista points (V) along the road offer sweeping views of the Cross Creek Valley.

Directions:

From U.S. 22 near the west edge of Wintersville, turn south onto County Road #34. Drive 3.5 miles, descending into the Cross Creek Valley. Turn right onto County Road #26, crossing a graffitied bridge, and proceed .8 mile southward and upward onto the next ridge. Turn left on Douglas Applegate Road. The Deer Run Trailhead lot will be .9 mile on your right.

Scene along the Deer Run Trail

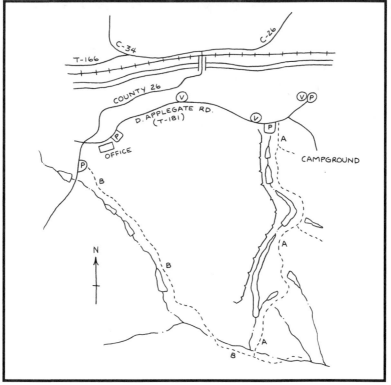

FERNWOOD STATE FOREST

30 HARRISON STATE FOREST

Distance: Day hikes of 1.5, 2.5 and 4.0 miles
Terrain: hilly; moderate grades

Secluded ponds, ridgetop meadows and wooded ravines characterize the 1344 acres of Harrison State Forest. Purchased in 1961, much of the preserve occupies land that was previously strip-mined. Today, the Forest is a popular area for hunting, fishing and camping.

Eight miles of hiking/bridal trails wind through the varied topography of Harrison State Forest. The eastern half of the preserve offers reliable parking, a good diversity of habitat and a combination of trails that lend themselves to day hikes.

Trail Routes:

Loop 1. This 2.5 mile hike begins at the parking area at the north end of Township Road 189 (see map). Hike northward, entering a broad grassland, and bear right at the trail intersection. The **Hilltop Trail (A)** leads along the eastern edge of the meadow and climbs toward the crest of the ridge. Meadowlarks and grassland sparrows are often spotted along the trail while hawks and kestrels patrol the area for rodents. White-tailed deer and red fox may be encountered here at dawn or dusk.

Bypass the cutoff to the **Lakeview Trail (B)** and continue northward to the highpoint (H) of the meadow. From here you can enjoy sweeping views of Harrison County and experience the windswept world of the prairie.

Return to the **Lakeview Trail** and turn left (east). This wide path enters a mixed woodland, curves to the south and descends along the edge of a basin. A series of woodland ponds will be noted on your left and stands of white pine rise above the trail. Near the bottom of the slope watch for a narrow footpath on your left which leads eastward between the largest ponds (see map). This is the **Lakeside Trail (C).**

A .5 mile hike takes you around the southernmost pond and back to the **Lakeview Trail (B)**. Climb to the Ronsheim Campground, off Township Road 189, turn right and ascend along the road to your car.

Loop 2. This 1.5 mile hike also begins at the parking lot at the north end of Township Road 189. Walk northward, entering the meadow, and bear left onto the **Deep Hollow Trail (D)**. This path is currently blazed with blue plastic streamers. After crossing the southern edge of the field, the trail cuts into the forest and descends along a drainage channel. Blocks of sandstone, dating from late in the Carboniferous Period, are strewn throughout the woodland and small ponds dot the forest.

At the bottom of the first ravine a side loop **(E)**, blazed with red streamers, leads southward. Bypass this cutoff and hike over a low ridge before the trail descends into Deep Hollow. Bear right at the next intersection (before reaching the creek) and walk northward along the shore of a picturesque woodland lake.

After a respite at this serene oasis, backtrack along the **Deep Hollow Trail** and turn right onto the spur loop **(E)**. This .5 mile path leads past another pond and curves back to the north, intersecting the **Deep Hollow Trail** at the south end of the meadow. Turn right and return to the parking area.

Combining the **Loop 1** and **Loop 2** routes obviously yields a total hike of 4.0 miles.

Directions:

From Cadiz, drive north on S.R. 9. Cross U.S. 22 and proceed another 3.4 miles. Turn right (east) on County Road 13 and drive 2.2. miles. Turn left on Township Road 189 and proceed .8 mile to the parking lot at its north end. Harrison State Forest is a public hunting area and hikers should exercise caution during hunting season.

Secluded woodland ponds characterize the area

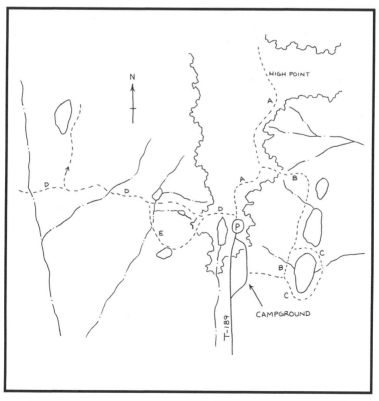

HARRISON STATE FOREST (EASTERN SECTION)

31 SALT FORK STATE PARK & WILDLIFE AREA

Distance: Day hikes of 1.8, 2.5 and 3.2 miles
Terrain: hilly; some steep areas

Just driving through the spacious realm of Salt Fork State Park and the adjacent Wildlife Management Area is a treat for the naturalist. Wildlife is abundant: white-tailed deer browse in the meadows, blue-birds hunt from the guardrails, wood-chucks forage along the roadways, great blue herons haunt the backwater shallows and turkey vultures soar above the Salt Fork basin. Beavers, once extirpated from the region, have again colonized the reservoir's feeder streams.

Impounding over 2900 acres of water surface, the dam across Salt Fork Creek was completed in 1967. Ohio's largest State Park now occupies the land between the lake's winding arms and the extensive Wildlife Management Unit, primarily north and east of the reservoir, brings the total area of this natural refuge to over 20,000 acres.

Despite the large size of the Salt Fork preserve, hiking trails are currently limited to rather short distances. The following routes offer an overview of the Park and Wildlife Area.

Trail Routes:
Buckeye Trail. The **Buckeye Trail**

(BT), blazed with blue slashes, cuts across the Salt Fork Wildlife Area, east of the reservoir. A 2.5 mile stretch of the trail cuts away from Road #59 and crosses a series of ridges; the following hike utilizes a 1.6 mile section of the **Buckeye Trail**, yielding a roundtrip distance of 3.2 miles.

Park at the Group Campground, .3 mile north of U.S. 22, on the west side of Road #59 (see map). Walk northward through the camping area and follow the **Buckeye Trail** as it curves to the left and descends into a creekbed. At the base of the ravine, cross the stream and wind through its boggy floodplain. You will soon begin a long, gradual ascent toward the north, eventually climbing onto a wooded knob. A clearing near the summit yields a broad view to the south and east.

Continuing northward, descend through the valley, cross an abandoned roadbed and climb onto the next ridge. Open woodland atop the ridge affords expansive views of the Salt Fork region. After a respite and picnic lunch on the summit, return to your car via the same route, completing a hike of 3.2 miles.

*Ridgetop view
from the
Buckeye Trail*

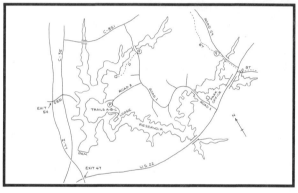

SALT FORK
STATE PARK
& WILDLIFE AREA

ROUTE ALONG
BUCKEYE TRAIL

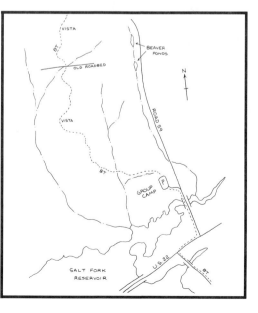

Morgan's Knob/Pine Crest. A combined route along three trails, all of which originate at the same parking area, yields a total hike of 2.5 miles. Proceed to the lot on Road #3, 1.6 miles south of its junction with Road #1 (see map).

Hike westward on the **Morgan's Knob Trail (A)** which cuts through a spruce plantation and then curves to the right. Bypass the cutoff to the **Morgan's Knob Loop (B)** and proceed westward, climbing steeply onto the ridge. A clearing at the top yields a spectacular view of the lake, the lodge area and the surrounding countryside.

Descend from the Knob and turn right onto the **Morgan's Knob Loop (B)**, blazed with red. The trail descends further along a deep ravine and then curves to the left, rounding a spur of land above the lake. Ascend gradually along another ravine and circle across its feeder streams. One of these plunges into the ravine via a waterfall.

Nearing the parking area, watch for the **Pine Crest Loop (C)**, blazed with blue, which cuts off to your right (see map). This 1 mile loop crosses through a pine woodland, winds above the lake and passes numerous outcroppings of sandstone. The latter date from the Pennsylvania Period, when shallow seas and extensive swampland covered much of eastern Ohio. Watch for woodchucks that often dig their burrows beneath these ledges of rock. Curving back to the north, complete the loop, turn right and follow the entry trail back to the parking lot.

Stone House Loop Trail (D). This 1.8 mile loop begins and ends at the parking lot along Road #1, 1.3 miles northwest of the junction with Road #3 and adjacent to a cove of Salt Fork Lake (see map). Cross the road, descend a short stairway and enter the forest, crossing two side streams. You will soon reach a fork in the trail and, since the route is an elongated loop, you can proceed in either direction. At the southern end of the loop, perched above Salt Fork Lake, is the Stone House. Built in 1837 for David B. Kennedy, the house was constructed with stone quarried from the immediate area. The structure is now listed on the National Register of Historic Places.

Directions:

Salt Fork State Park is just east of I-77 and north of U.S. 22, approximately 8 miles northeast of Cambridge, Ohio. From I-77, take Exit 47 and drive east on U.S. 22 for 6 miles to the Park's main entrance (Road #1). Park Road #59 is another mile to the east. Refer to the maps for the location of parking areas.

Looking southeast from Morgan's Knob

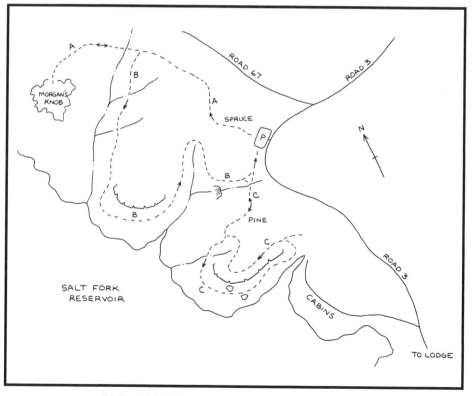

MORGAN'S KNOB / PINE CREST TRAILS

V. HIKING AREAS OF SOUTHWEST OHIO

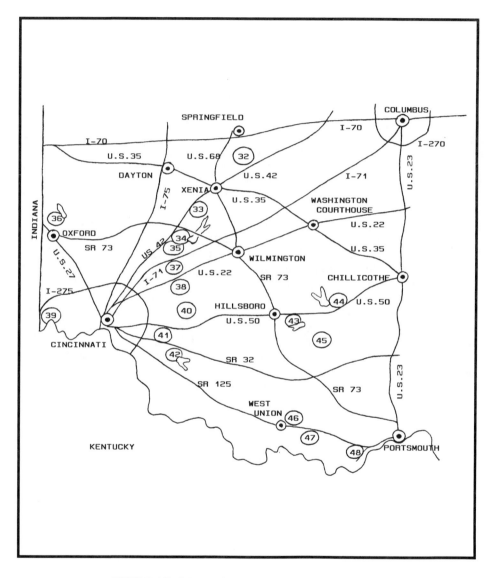

HIKING AREAS OF SOUTHWEST OHIO

32 CLIFTON GORGE PRESERVE/JOHN BRYAN STATE PARK

Distance: 5.2 miles
Terrain: rolling; few steep areas & stairs

Few areas in Ohio can match the scenic beauty, geologic history and botanical diversity of Clifton Gorge. Carved from Silurian bedrock by a torrent of glacial meltwater, the Gorge now channels the upper Little Miami River.

Plants that once flourished in the periglacial zone of the late Pleistocene still cling to the shaded walls of the chasm. The north-facing ravines are especially rich in glacial relict vegetation. Among these species are hemlock, Canadian yew, arborvitae and mountain maple. Over 340 species of wildflower have been found in the gorge and the cool, moist environment offers ideal conditions for 16 varieties of fern. Red squirrels scamper among the hemlocks while eight species of salamander inhabit moist recesses of the Gorge.

The narrow, eastern end of the Gorge is protected within the Clifton Gorge State Nature Preserve, dedicated in October, 1973. Stretching west from this refuge, the 750 acres of John Bryan State Park encompass another segment of the river channel. Access to the excellent trail network within these preserves is via parking areas at Clifton, Ohio, or within the State Park (see map). The following route covers 5.2 miles and winds past many of the scenic highlights of Clifton Gorge.

Trail Route:

Park in the Jackson St. lot, adjacent to the Upper Gorge Overlook (1). Follow the **Narrows Trail (A)** as it winds to the north and then curves westward along the rim of the Gorge. Three more overlooks (2,3,4) provide spectacular views into the chasm and across to the Scientific Preserve. The latter, closed to the public, harbors the greatest concentration of glacial relict vegetation within Clifton Gorge.

Bypass the stairway that leads into the Gorge and pass another parking access trail, on your right. Cross through a gate and, at the fork in the trail, bear left onto the **North Rim Trail (B)** which runs for 2 miles atop the steep cliffs. Bypass more side trails that lead into the Gorge or up to the **Orton Trail (C)**. Continue westward on the **North Rim Trail**, entering John Bryan State Park, where stands of chinquapin oak thrive on the dry, sun-exposed slopes. You will eventually emerge onto a roadway; turn left and descend to a riverside picnic area.

Head back upstream along a wide, level trail **(D)** that follows the abandoned bed of the Pittsburgh-Cincinnati stagecoach route. Continue eastward along the north bank of the river, bypassing two bridges that cross to the south side. Silurian dolomites are the predominant rock formations along the steep walls of the gorge. Seams of less-resistant shale erode more quickly and cause large "slump-blocks" of dolomite to tumble into the river channel. The most prominant of these is "Steamboat Rock (7)." Numerous springs and waterfalls splash into the gorge from its rugged walls and offer moist retreats for the resident amphibians.

Crossing back into the State Nature Preserve, continue eastward along the **John L. Rich Trail (E)**, also called the **North Gorge Trail**. This scenic stretch passes the "Blue Hole (5)," "Amphitheater Falls (6)" and "Steamboat Rock (7)." Ascend the stairway at the end of the trail and return to the Jackson St. parking lot via the **Narrows Trail (A)**.

Directions:

Clifton Gorge extends westward from Clifton, Ohio, running south of S.R. 343. John Bryan State Park also lies south of S.R. 343, between Yellow Springs and Clifton, and is accessed via S.R. 310. To reach the area from I-70, take Exit #54 and drive south on S.R. 72 to Clifton (approximately 6.8 miles).

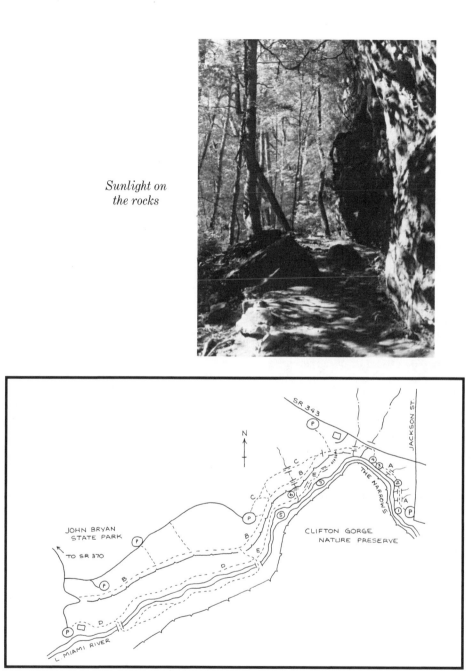

*Sunlight on
the rocks*

CLIFTON GORGE / JOHN BRYAN S.P.

From the Dayton area, take Exit #20 from I-675 and head east on Dayton-Yellow Springs Road for 6.6 miles. Turn left for 1 block on S.R. 68 and then right (east) on S.R. 43. Proceed 3.3 miles to Jackson St., in Clifton, and turn right; the parking lot will soon appear on your right.

33 SPRING VALLEY WILDLIFE AREA

Distance: Day hikes of 2.0 and 3.6 miles
Terrain: flat

Spring Valley Wildlife Area is an 842 acre preserve in the Little Miami Valley, approximately 6 miles northeast of Waynesville. Its 80 acre lake and adjacent marsh are popular destinations for naturalists and hunters alike.

Purchase of the refuge began during the early 1950s and the preserve is now managed by District Five of the Division of Wildlife, Ohio Department of Natural Resources. Access to the trail system is via parking areas off Roxanna-New Burlington Road, off Pence-Jones Road or at the south end of the lake (see map). The terrain is flat and the wide trail, despite its course through a perpetual wetland, is remarkably dry throughout the year. Insect repellent is strongly recommended during the warmer months.

Trail Route:

A 2 mile loop trail winds around the lake and through the marsh, providing unusual access to such an extensive wetland. Canada geese, mallards and wood ducks nest at the preserve and migrant waterfowl are abundant in spring and fall. Ospreys often stop to fish on the lake during their migrations through Ohio. Ring-necked pheasants and bobwhite quail forage on open grasslands and numerous song-

birds are attracted to the moist woodlands. Resident mammals include muskrats, mink, woodchucks, skunk and white-tailed deer. Botanists are drawn to the wooded swamp northwest of the lake, where skunk cabbage blooms in late winter.

Should you choose to limit your hike to the 2 mile lake/marsh loop, park at the access lot off Pence-Jones Road or in the large lot at the south end of the lake.

Your total hike can be increased to 3.6 miles by parking at the south end of Road #1 (see map) and walking along the east bank of the Little Miami River to the south end of Spring Valley Lake. This .8 mile trail segment is actually the northernmost section of the **Little Miami Scenic Trail**, which parallels the river from the eastern edge of Cincinnati to the Spring Valley Wildlife Area, a distance of 44 miles. Your roundtrip hike along the river, combined with the 2 mile loop around the lake, yields a total hike of 3.6 miles.

Directions:

From I-71, take Exit #45 and drive west on S.R. 73 to Waynesville (approximately 9 miles). Turn right (north) on U.S. 42 and proceed 5.7 miles. Turn right (east) on Roxanna-New Burlington Road and park in one of the lots illustrated on the map.

March sunshine thaws the wetland.

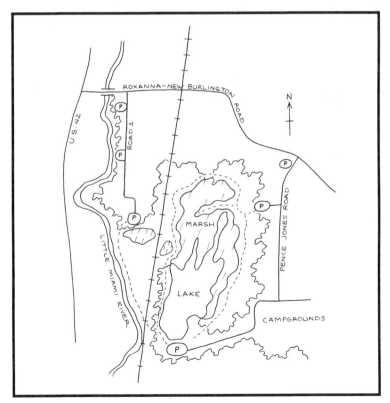

SPRING VALLEY WILDLIFE AREA

34 CAESAR CREEK STATE PARK

Distance: Day hikes of 3.6, 5.0, 5.6 and 13.4 miles
Terrain: rolling; few steep areas

Caesar Creek Lake is a 2800 acre flood-control reservoir in the Little Miami watershed. Since its completion, in 1978, the Lake has been a popular destination for boaters and fishermen. The adjacent 7720 acre State Park, characterized by open woodlands, meadows and parcels of forest, offers other recreational opportunities.

Trail Routes:

A 13.4 mile hiking trail winds around the southern section of the reservoir (the area south of S.R. 73). Access to this loop is via parking areas at the Visitor Center, at Furnas Shores, at Fifty Springs or at Wellman Meadows (see map). The majority of the trail crosses flat or gently rolling terrain though some sections, especially near the inlet streams, are a bit steep. The 13.4 mile trail is actually the shortest route around the southern section of Caesar Creek Lake; additional side loops at Fifty Springs, Wellman Meadows and at the Saddle Dam area, bring the total circuit to 18.8 miles. The **Buckeye Trail**, blazed with blue paint, utilizes the western half of the loop. Please refer to the map for the layout and sectional mileage of the trail system.

Shorter day hikes are more reasonable for most hikers. The following routes, utilizing sections of the longer loop, are suggested:

A. Furnas Shores to West Lookout Point. This gentle but undulating hike leads from the Furnas Shores parking area to a natural lookout above a wide cove along the Lake's western rim. The route, which coincides with a section of the **Buckeye Trail (BT)**, crosses open woodlands, dense cedar groves and second growth forest. After hiking approximately 2 miles, you will reach a straight, level section of the trail, running high above the Lake (see map);

this is one of the reservoir's support dikes. Just south of the dike area you will wind around the upper reaches of a deep ravine and soon come to a fork in the trail. The main trail (and Buckeye Trail) angle to the right and loop around a wide cove. Turn left for a short walk out to a lookout which offers a broad view of Caesar Creek Lake. Return to Furnas Shores via the same route for a total hike of 5.0 miles.

B. Fifty Springs to Pioneer Village. This hike begins at the first parking lot along Fifty Springs Road and winds southward for 1.8 miles to Pioneer Village. The latter is a collection of Quaker buildings that date from the late 18th and early 19th Centuries. The structures were obtained and renovated by the Caesar Creek Pioneer Village Association in an effort to preserve the cultural heritage of Ohio's rural past. Completing the roundtrip to Fifty Springs, your hike will total 3.6 miles.

C. Wellman Meadows to Visitor Center. This moderately strenuous hike starts at the first Wellman Meadows parking lot and snakes around the southern end of Caesar Creek Lake, crossing Flat Fork inlet and then ascending to the top of the Dam wall. Proceeding to the Visitor Center, just north of the Dam, your one-way distance is 2.8 miles. The Center houses the Corps of Engineers offices, a theater and exhibits that illustrate the natural history of the Caesar Creek region. An overlook of the Dam area is located behind the building. Return to Wellman Meadows via the same route for a total hike of 5.6 miles.

Directions:

Caesar Creek Lake and State Park extend north and south from S.R. 73, approximately 3 miles east of Waynesville (or 4 miles west of I-71). Refer to the map for the location of parking areas.

A view from the east shore

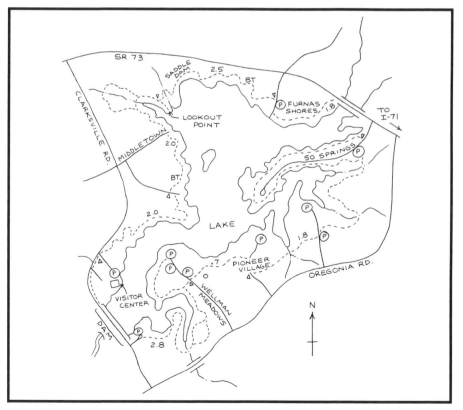

CAESAR CREEK BACKPACK TRAIL

35 CAESAR CREEK GORGE STATE NATURE PRESERVE

Distance: 2 miles
Terrain: rolling; few steep areas

Meltwater from the Pleistocene glaciers carved a deep valley through the rolling countryside of Greene, Clinton and Warren Counties in southwest Ohio. Later drained by Caesar Creek, a major tributary of the Little Miami River, much of the valley is now inundated by a flood-control reservoir (see Hike #34).

Below the dam, the gorge has remained in its pre-reservoir state. Forested ravines rise 180 feet above the stream which has cut steep cliffs through the Ordovician bedrock. Deep in the gorge, a floodplain woodland stretches along the valley floor.

The 483 acre Nature Preserve was dedicated in January, 1975, to protect this scenic and biologically rich area. The following trail route winds through the varied habitats of the refuge.

Trail Route:

Follow the wide, grassy trail that leads north from the parking lot. You will soon intersect an old jeep trail and encounter your first view of the Caesar Creek Gorge. Turn right and follow the jeep trail as it slowly climbs eastward. After hiking approximately 100 yards, angle to the left onto an earthen trail that descends onto the floodplain of Caesar Creek. Winding across this moist woodland, the narrow trail is hemmed in by dense foliage during the summer months. Insects and spiders are abundant.

You will eventually arrive along the south bank of Caesar Creek and then wind upstream. Short side trails lead to the water's edge. Watch for darters in the cool, clear stream. After hiking ½ mile upstream, you will angle back into the dense woodland. At the eastern end of the loop a spur trail cuts back to the creek while the main trail curves southwestward and soon widens into a grassy path. Reaching higher ground, the trail enters a wet meadow where wildflowers abound during the warmer months.

Skirt the eastern rim of this clearing (see map) and pick up the wide, rocky trail that leads into the hillside forest. A long, steady climb taxes your body but offers expansive views into the gorge from late fall to early spring. At the top of the ridge the trail leaves the forest and meanders across open fields. These successional meadows, recovering from earlier cultivation, are slowly filling with thickets and cedar groves. Wildflowers adorn the area in summer, especially from August through September.

Continue westward as the trail re-enters the woodland and gradually descends to the parking area.

Directions:

From the intersection of U.S. 42 and Ohio 73 (at Waynesville, Ohio), head east on Route 73, drive .4 mile and turn left onto Smith Road. This small, two-lane road curves back to the west and deadends into Corwin Road. Turn left (south) on Corwin Road and drive 2.5 miles to the Preserve, on your left. A section of the Little Miami Scenic Trail parallels Corwin Road in this area (see Hike #38).

A view into the Gorge

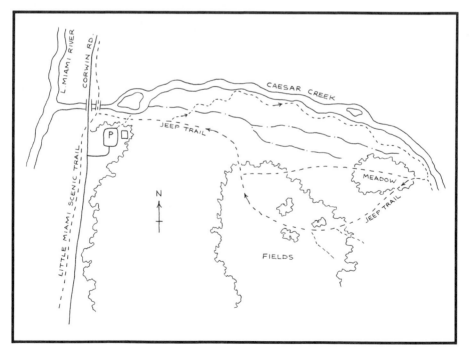

CAESAR CREEK GORGE PRESERVE

36 HUESTON WOODS STATE PARK & NATURE PRESERVE

Distance: 3.2 miles
Terrain: rolling; few steep areas

When Daniel Boone and his cohorts reached the Ohio Valley, over 95% of our State was cloaked by virgin hardwood forest. Since then, farming, timber production, the iron industry and clearance for urban sprawl has reduced forest cover to but a small fraction of Ohio's total acreage. Most of the woodlands we see today are second or third growth forest.

Thanks to the foresight of the Matthew Hueston family, a 200 acre parcel of virgin hardwood has been protected in Preble and Butler Counties. The Huestons acquired the land about 1800 and, after 140 years of stewardship, turned it over to the State of Ohio in 1941. The virgin forest now lies within Hueston Woods State Park and stretches along the west shore of Acton Lake. The latter reservoir was formed by the damming of Four Mile Creek in 1956.

Designated a National Natural Landmark in 1967, the protected woods is a classic remnant of the beech-maple forests that once covered most of western and northern Ohio. The tall hardwoods and mature understory create a cathedral-like atmosphere. Woodland wildflowers flourish in April and early May before the dense canopy closes out the sun and shade-tolerant seedlings of the beech and maple giants carpet the forest floor.

A State Nature Preserve since 1973, the Woods are accessed from several parking areas in Hueston Woods State Park. The following route combines a hike along the west shore of Acton Lake with a tour of the virgin hardwood forest, permitting close study of this natural timecapsule.

Trail Route:
From the Acton Lake Picnic Area (see Directions on next page), follow the old jeep trail that leads toward the Dam from the end of the turn-around loop. Angle left onto the **West Shore Trail (A)** and hike northward above the lake. The trail undulates through the forest, crossing numerous side streams. Views of the lake are constant and the State Park lodge dominates the scene along the eastern shore.

After hiking approximately .6 mile you will enter the State Nature Preserve and another .5 mile brings you to the intersection with the **Blue Heron Trail (B)**. Turn right, cross the creek and bear left, continuing toward the north. At the next intersection, bear right along the **West Shore Trail (A)** and you will soon emerge near the Sugar House where maple syrup is distilled each spring.

Continue northward along the combined route of the **West Shore Trail** and the **Sugarbush Trail (C)**. Bypass side trails that lead to the lakeshore and ascend onto the hillside via an earthen stairway. Bear left at the fork, staying on the **Sugarbush Trail**, and hike westward between two ravines. Crossing over Brown Road you will enter one of the more open and beautiful sections of the Preserve. Huge beech, maple and ash trees tower above the relatively sparse, shade-tolerant plants of the forest floor.

Bear right onto the **Blue Heron Trail (B)**, cut through a parking area and continue eastward, descending toward the lake. At the bottom of the slope, turn right onto the **West Shore Trail (A)** and return to the Acton Lake Picnic Area. Your round-trip hike along the lakeshore and through the Forest Preserve has covered 3.2 miles.

*In the
"Big Woods"*

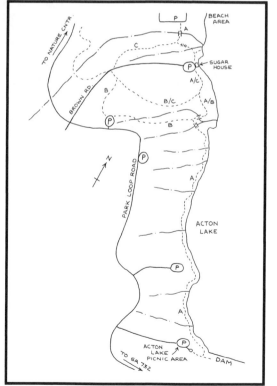

Directions:

Hueston Woods State Park lies north of S.R. 732, approximately 5 miles northeast of Oxford. From the Park entrance (which is just west of S.R. 177), proceed along the entry road for .4 mile and bear left onto the loop road that encircles Acton Lake. Drive 2 miles, crossing Four Mile Creek below the Dam, ascend the next hill and turn right into the Acton Lake Picnic Area.

After your hike, plan a visit to Hueston Wood's Nature Center, north of the Forest Preserve and Beach Area. The Center includes a rehabilitation facility for regional birds of prey.

**HUESTON WOODS PRESERVE
AND WEST SHORE TRAIL**

37 FT. ANCIENT STATE MEMORIAL

Distance: 3.2 miles
Terrain: mostly flat but steep ascent and descent of ridge

Remnants of prehistoric human culture are found throughout southern Ohio. Most renowned are the relics of the Adena and Hopewell Indians, often called the "mound builders," who settled along river valleys and constructed elaborate earthworks.

Ft. Ancient State Memorial, managed by the Ohio Historical Society, protects a 100 acre Hopewell "fortress," high above the banks of the Little Miami River. Now thought to have been ceremonial in nature, the earthen-walled structure is divided into southern, middle and northern sections. The Hopewells settled in the valley around 100 B.C. and established a culture based on hunting, trading and primitive farming. Why they disappeared from the region around 600 A.D. remains a mystery. Six centuries later after their departure, the area was occupied by the Ft. Ancient Indians, more advanced farmers who cultivated corn on the floodplain of the Little Miami.

The entire Ft. Ancient Memorial encompasses 746 acres across the east flank of the river valley. The "fort" itself spreads atop the ridge, 240 feet above the level of the stream. The following route yields a 3.2 mile hike through the Preserve.

Trail Route:

Park in the Ft. Ancient Access Lot along S.R. 350, just east of the Little Miami River. Walk eastward along the road for approximately 50 yards and turn right on the abandoned bed of the Little Miami Railroad, now the **Little Miami Scenic Trail (A)**. Hike downstream along this wide path and proceed .6 mile to a sidestream, evidenced by wooden rails along the **Little Miami Trail**. The **North Overlook Trail (B)** to Ft. Ancient's south fort enters the forest at this point (see map).

Turn left onto the **North Overlook Trail** and begin a steep climb to the ridgetop, gaining 240 feet of elevation in just over .25 mile. The trail follows high ground between divergent ravines and offers extensive views during the colder months. Pass the cutoff to the **Terrace Trail (D)** and continue up to the North Overlook (1). From its deck, at an elevation of 894 feet, you are treated to a spectacular view of the Little Miami Valley as it curves in from the north. The I-71 bridge, highest in Ohio, is clearly visible in the distance.

Hike southward along the **Earthworks Trail (C)**, paralleling the ridgetop mounds of the South Fort. Winding to the east you will pass a wooden bridge (2) that crosses the mounds and leads to the **Terrace Trail**. Bypass this bridge and bear left, entering a swath of forest and crossing through two deep ravines. Exit the woodland and proceed out to the South Overlook (3). The view from this site, more expansive in winter, extends across the River and southward through the valley.

Backtrack to the junction with the **Terrace Trail (D)**, cross the earthworks via the bridge and begin a short but steep descent. The trail soon angles to the right and winds along the valley wall, crossing several small drainages. Deer often browse on this sunny slope, bounding away as you approach. Views of the Little Miami are constant during the winter months.

After hiking about .5 mile along the terrace, you will curve to the right and intersect the **North Overlook Trail (B)**. Turn left, descend to the **Little Miami Trail (A)** and return to the parking area.

Directions:

Take Exit #36 from I-71 (Warren Co. Rd. 7). Proceed to the east side of the highway and take an immediate right onto a road that parallels I-71 for a short distance and then curves to the east. Drive 2 miles and

Almost 4 miles of earthworks enclose Fort Ancient.

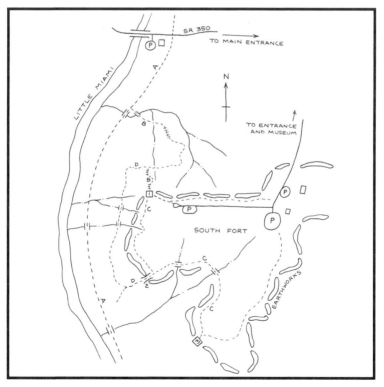

TRAILS OF THE SOUTH FORT

turn right on S.R. 350. Bypass the auto entrance to Ft. Ancient and descend into the Little Miami Gorge. The "Ft. Ancient Access" lot will be on your left, just before reaching the River. After your hike, plan a visit to Ft. Ancient's museum which houses artifacts from the prehistoric Indian cultures.

38 LITTLE MIAMI SCENIC TRAIL

Distance: Day hikes of 2.5 and 7.0 miles; numerous alternative hikes as per map
Terrain: flat

The continued loss of open space and wildlife habitat, coupled with an increased interest in aerobic exercise, spawned the creation of the Rails-to-Trails Conservancy in 1985. This national, non-profit organization is devoted to the conversion of abandoned railroad beds to hiking, biking and bridal paths. To date, the Conservancy has coordinated the conversion of over 2400 miles of former rail lines to earthen or paved trails. According to the Organization, 2000-4000 miles of railroad are abandoned annually and over 160,000 miles of idle track are laced across this country. The potential benefits from their effort is thus enormous. Your support is encouraged and the Ohio Chapter's address and phone number are listed in Appendix II.

A prime example of the rail-to-trail concept is the **Little Miami Scenic Trail** in southwest Ohio. Following the abandoned bed of the defunct Little Miami Railroad (circa 1840s), this 44 mile trail winds along the River from Greater Cincinnati to the Spring Valley Wildlife Area, northeast of Waynesville. The 14 mile stretch between Loveland and Morrow has been paved for use by cyclists and plans are underway to also pave the 8 mile section from Milford to Loveland. In addition, the Trail will eventually extend northward to Springfield, yielding a total distance of 72 miles. The **Buckeye Trail** utilizes most of the route from Milford to Spring Valley.

While the trail parallels the Little Miami River, it is not always adjacent to the stream. Forest and farmlands intervene in some areas and views of the River vary accordingly. The following day hikes are suggested; alternative routes may be planned by referring to the map on page 101 which depicts sectional mileage along the Trail.

Trail Routes:
Loveland to Foster (7 miles roundtrip). This hike utilizes the southernmost 3.5 miles of the paved section. Often congested with cyclists on warm weather weekends, it is best undertaken on off-season weekdays. Much of the route stays near the River but vistas are broader in winter when leaves do not obstruct the view. The Loveland trailhead, perhaps the most popular access point for the **Little Miami Trail**, lies amidst an appealing collection of shops. At the north end of the hike, the small town of Foster camps along the west bank, just beyond the picturesque U.S. 22 bridge.

Fort Ancient to Mathers Mill (2.5 miles roundtrip). Winding through the most scenic stretch of the Little Miami gorge, this wide, earthen path crosses under Ohio's highest bridge, the I-71 span. The Little Miami, designated a State and National Scenic River in 1968, remains in view through much of the route and flotillas of canoes grace the scene during the warmer months. Forested walls rise 250 feet above the River, creating updrafts for hawks and vultures that soar overhead.

Directions:
The **Little Miami Scenic Trail** may be accessed at Spring Valley Wildlife Area, Caesar Creek Gorge Nature Preserve and Fort Ancient as described in Hikes 33, 35 and 37, respectively. The Loveland trailhead is reached by taking Exit #52 from I-275, north of Cincinnati and east of I-71. Drive north on Loveland-Madeira Road, proceed 3 miles and turn right on Loveland Ave. Cross the bridge, proceed another block and turn left on Railroad Ave. which

A summer scene along the River

leads to a large parking area along the Trail.

The Mathers Mill Access is reached by taking Exit #36 from I-71. Drive west on Warren County Road 7 for 1.5 miles, descending to the River. The lot is on the east bank, just south of the bridge. To reach the Morrow trailhead, take Exit #32 from I-71 and follow S.R. 123 southeast for 5.5 miles into Morrow. Turn right on U.S. 22, proceed 4 blocks and turn right on Center St. The large parking area stretches south from Morrow's old railroad depot.

In addition to the Rails-to-Trails Conservancy, the Ohio Department of Natural Resources, Little Miami, Inc., Rivers Unlimited and the Ohio Chapter of the Nature Conservancy have all been involved with the protection of the Little Miami River and its Valley. These vital organizations are listed in Appendix II.

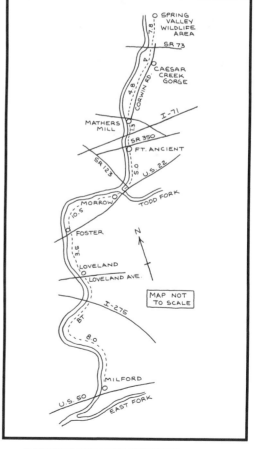

LITTLE MIAMI SCENIC TRAIL

39 SHAWNEE LOOKOUT PARK

Distance: Day hikes of 1.5 and 3.3 miles
Terrain: hilly; some steep areas

Hamilton County, encompassing Greater Cincinnati, boasts an excellent system of Parks. Of these, Shawnee Lookout Park, overlooking the confluence of the Ohio and Great Miami Rivers, offers an attractive mix of scenery, vistas, human history and good hiking.

Stretched across a ridgetop, just east of the Great Miami floodplain, the area has been the site of human habitation for over 15,000 years. Its first residents were likely the Paleo-hunters, nomadic people who followed herds of mammoths and bison during the Pleistocene Epoch. Hopewell Indians, migrating into the region about 300 B.C., constructed the earthen "fort" and burial mounds that characterize the southern end of the ridge. Modern tribes, including Miami and Shawnee Indians, settled along the ridge by the early 1700s.

Through the efforts of the Miami Purchase Association, this natural and archeologic treasure was added to the Hamilton County Park District in 1967. Three excellent hiking trails are located within the Park and guide brochures are available at the ranger station. The following day hikes are suggested.

Trail Routes:

Miami Fort Trail (A). This 1.5 mile loop begins and ends at the parking area located at the southwestern end of the Park's central drive. From the lot, ascend through the forest via a wide path. Near the top of the ridge you will enter the Miami Fort, a clearing surrounded by long, earthen mounds. The latter have since been colonized by forest vegetation.

Bear right at the fork in the trail and wind along the western edge of the Shawnee ridge. Overlooks provide sweeping views of the Great Miami Valley, including extensive wetlands known as "the Oxbow." Oxbow Inc., listed in Appendix II, is a local organization working to protect these wetlands from industrial development. The marshlands, ponds and flooded fields of the Valley are vital staging grounds for waterfowl and shorebirds. Bald eagles, ospreys, cormorants and an occasional peregrine falcon are spotted at the Oxbow during migrations.

Nearing the south end of the ridge a spur trail leads out to the "Shawnee Lookout" overlooking the confluence of the Ohio and Great Miami Rivers. Barges ply the Ohio and the I-275 bridge spans the River just west of the Indiana border. Return to the primary loop and turn right, soon dipping through a ravine and climbing onto the south edge of the ridge. Winding toward the northeast, the trail re-enters the Miami Fort and merges with the entry route. Descend to the parking area, completing a hike of 1.5 miles.

Forest has reclaimed the earthen mounds.

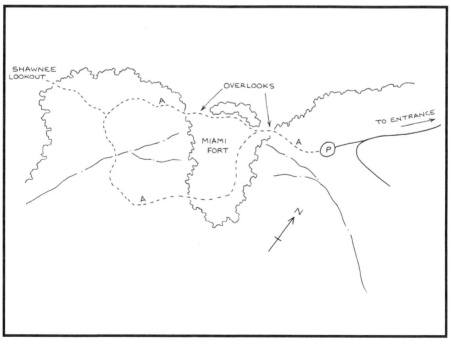

THE MIAMI FORT TRAIL

Little Turtle and **Blue Jacket Trails**. The combination of these two loops, both of which originate at the same parking area, yields a total hike of 3.3 miles. Park in the lot on the north side of the central road, approximately .6 mile in from the Park entrance. Cross the road and find the **Little Turtle Trail (B)** which enters the forest behind a playground. Named for a Chief of the Miami Indian tribe, this two mile loop initially angles toward the southwest and skirts an open meadow. Continue straight ahead through the trail intersection, snaking into a ravine and then climbing onto the next ridge. At the crest of the ridge the forest opens up to yield a spectacular view of the Ohio River, backed by the hills of northern Kentucky.

After enjoying the view, hike southward along the ridge. The trail soon curves to the right and returns to the previous intersection. Turn left and hike back to the parking area.

Cross through the lot and pick up the **Blue Jacket Trail (C)**, a 1.3 mile loop named for a Chief of the Shawnee tribe. Descend through the forest, cross a power line swath and watch for a fork in the trail. Bear left, cross through a second power line clearing and descend into a deep ravine. Climbing onto the next ridge the trail soon reaches a clearing which offers a broad view of the forested hills that line the Ohio River. Angling to the northeast, the path climbs higher and reaches a second overlook; before you is the fertile floodplain of the Great Miami River, home to the Oxbow wetlands discussed in the **Miami Fort** hike.

Continue along the crest of the ridge, curving to the southeast and re-crossing the power line swaths. White-tailed deer often browse in these clearings and are best observed at dawn or dusk. A gentle ascent along the entry trail brings you back to the parking area.

Directions:

From I-275, on the west side of Cincinnati, take Exit #16. Turn right (east) on U.S. 50 and drive 7.4 miles into Cleves, Ohio. Turn right onto Mt. Nebo Road, proceed 1½ blocks and turn right on Miami St. which curves to the left, paralleling the Great Miami River, and becomes Lawrenceburg Road. Drive approximately 4 miles to the Park entrance, on your left. A daily usage fee of $1.00 per vehicle is charged.

The majestic Ohio River from the Little Turtle Trail

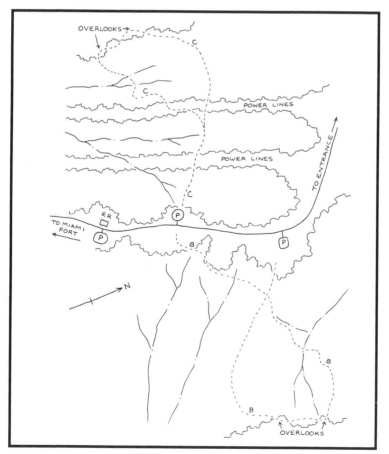

LITTLE TURTLE & BLUE JACKET TRAILS

40 STONELICK STATE PARK

Distance: 5.4 miles roundtrip
Terrain: flat/gently rolling

Stonelick, characterized by mixed woodlands and meadows flanking a 181 acre lake, is one of our smaller State Parks. Nevertheless, it harbors 7 miles of hiking trails and is a popular area for picnics and fishing. The lake's backwater habitat can be excellent for birdwatching.

The route below yields a 5.4 mile hike through some of the Park's more interesting topography. Due to the relatively flat terrain and poor drainage, sections of the trail can be sloppy, especially after periods of wet weather. In addition, wood ticks seem especially abundant at Stonelick and a repellent is advised during the warmer months. For these reasons, I suggest a late-autumn or winter visit to Stonelick State Park.

From the Park office, follow Lake Drive (Road #1) northeastward into the Park. Drive .9 mile and turn left into a one-way lane that curves back around a lakeside picnic area. Park in the first lot on your right.

Trail Route:

The trailhead for the 1.0 mile **Lakeview Trail (A)** is at the east end of the picnic area (see map). Cross a small drainage and hike eastward along the south shore of Stonelick Lake. Stands of white pine and red cedar yield a pleasing fragrance and contrast with the dominant hardwood forest. After hugging the shoreline for ¼ mile, the trail turns southward, looping around an inlet of the lake. It then makes a beeline through the woods, paralleling a feeder stream.

Just before emerging onto Lake Drive, angle to the left on the .7 mile **Southwoods Trail (B)**. This path winds past large beech trees and shagbark hickory, crossing multiple drainages along the way. Watch for

pileated woodpeckers in this area.

Upon reaching Lake Drive, turn right for about 25 yards and pick up the **Red Fox Trail (C)** on the opposite side of the road. This 2.0 mile route winds through swampy woodlands that encircle the backwaters of Stonelick Lake. Hike into the forest for a short distance and bear right at the fork in the trail. Entering a zone of swamp forest, the trail can be overgrown and boggy during the spring and summer months. After negotiating this wetland you will reach a somewhat higher and drier woodland and soon cross a narrow roadbed (see map).

The trail eventually curves to the northwest and diverges. Bear left, returning to the straight, narrow roadbed. Turn right onto this wide path, gradually descending to the backwater marshlands of Stonelick Lake. Mallards, wood ducks, herons and numerous songbirds are drawn to this moist, buggy environment. Resident mammals include mink, muskrat, skunk and white-tailed deer.

Return eastward along the straight, wide path, passing two ponds on your right. Watch for the west arm of the **Red Fox Trail**, a short distance beyond the second pond. Turn right, cross through the swamp forest again and return to the entry trail. Retrace your route along the **Southwoods** and **Lakeview Trails**, completing a round-trip hike of 5.4 miles.

Directions:

Stonelick State park is on S.R. 727, 2 miles southwest of Edenton. From Milford, Ohio, drive east on S.R. 131. Proceed 8.5 miles and angle left onto S.R. 727. Drive 3 miles to the Park entrance, on your right. From the Park office, follow Lake Drive to the parking lot, as described above.

Stonelick's backwater marsh

STONELICK STATE PARK (EASTERN SECTION)

41 CINCINNATI NATURE CENTER

Distance: 3.5 miles
Terrain: rolling; some hilly areas with moderate grades

The Cincinnati Nature Center, located east of Milford, Ohio, offers an excellent setting for day hikes. The Center's 750 acres sprawl atop the East Fork Valley and are accessed by an extensive network of trails. Well-maintained and easily followed, the trails radiate from the Rowe Interpretive Center (A), which houses the refuge offices, a nature-oriented bookstore and informative exhibits.

The map included in this guide is limited to the areas covered by the day-hike route that I have chosen. Numbered intersections correspond with markers used at the Preserve and a more complete map is provided by the Nature Center. The following 3.5 mile hike winds through the refuge and takes you past the varied habitats that characterize the area.

Trail Route:

Start behind the Rowe Interpretive Center (A) and hike along the southwestern edge of Powel Crosley Lake (B) via a boardwalk. Partially ringed by a marsh, this oasis provides favored habitat for Canada geese, red-winged blackbirds, mink and migrant waterfowl. Proceed to intersection #5, turn right and wind into the gorge of Avery Run. Angle to the right and follow the stream as it flows toward the East Fork of the Little Miami River.

After crossing and re-crossing the creek you will emerge from the forest at the edge of a meadow (C); this is intersection #9. The meadow harbors a vast array of wildflowers during the summer months and attracts eastern bluebirds throughout the year. Hike along the eastern edge of the clearing and re-enter the forest, climbing the valley wall via a series of switchbacks. At intersection #12, turn left and loop around to intersection #13. Turn right and

exit the forest near a marsh-lined pond (D), a haven for amphibians during the warmer months of the year.

Cut across the center of a crop field (E) and enter a dense woodland at intersection #17. Pass a bird blind on your left and hike northward, paralleling the Center's entry road. Cross through an auxillary parking area and pick up the trail at intersection #19. Bear right at the next three intersections, passing behind a private homestead and to the east of Woodland Pond (F).

A gradual descent takes you across Tealtown Road and then the route climbs back into the forest. Turn left onto the spur trail at intersection #22 for a short walk to an overlook of the East Fork Valley. Return to the main trail, turn left and wind along the rim of the valley; overlooks are spaced along the way and the route cuts in and out of the forest as it curves toward the east. After passing intersection #25 the trail turns southward, crosses a hayfield (G) and arrives at Willow Pond (H). Continue along the edge of the field, re-cross Tealtown Road and follow the Center's entry road to the parking area.

Directions:

Follow I-275 to the east side of Cincinnati and take Exit #63-B. Drive east for 1.2 miles on S.R. 32 and turn left on Gleneste-Withamsville Road. Drive .4 mile, turn right on Old S.R. 74 and proceed .25 mile to Tealtown Road. Turn left and drive approximately 3 miles to the Center, on your left.

The Cincinnati Nature Center is open to the public on weekdays but is reserved for members on weekends and holidays. For information regarding membership, contact the Center at the address listed in Appendix II.

Powel Crosley Lake

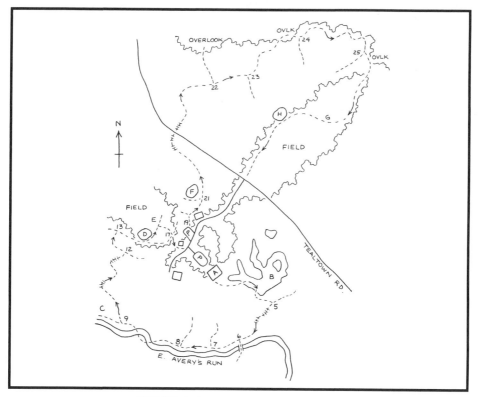

CINCINNATI NATURE CENTER

42 EAST FORK STATE PARK

Distance: Day hikes of 5.0 and 12.0 miles
Terrain: hilly; some steep areas

Completed in 1978, William Harsha Lake was created for flood control, water storage and recreation along the East Fork of the Little Miami River. Surrounding this 2100 acre reservoir is East Fork State Park, 8000 acres of forest, meadow and open woodlands.

The Park provides two major hiking trails. The 35 mile Backcountry Trail (BCT), now designated the **Steve Newman Worldwalker Perimeter Trail**, circles the reservoir. The trail is named in honor of the Bethel, Ohio, native who circumnavigated the globe on foot. Also open to horseback riders, four overnight shelters are spaced along its route. Access to the **Backcountry Trail**, which is blazed with green, is via the Main Trailhead (T) lot or via the large parking area adjacent to the Campground Office (CO).

East Fork's **Backpack Trail (BPT)**, blazed with red-orange slashes, winds for 12 miles through parkland south of the reservoir. This trail is reserved for hikers (no horses) and is accessed via the Main Trailhead (T). Side trails at East Fork are blazed with white and the **Buckeye Trail (BT)**, which cuts across northern sections of the Park, is blazed with blue.

Trail Routes:

Since the primary trail loops are a bit too long for day hikes, the following routes are suggested:

Backpack Trail/Backcountry Trail Loop. Perhaps the best day hike at East Fork State Park is a 5 mile loop that combines the western section of the **Backpack Trail (BPT)**, a connecting trail to Overnight Area #1 and a short return along the **Backcountry Trail (BCT)**.

From the Main Trailhead (T) parking lot, off the south entrance road, follow the **Backpack Trail** northward into the woods. Blazed with red-orange slashes, the trail is well designed and easily followed. After crossing through a deep ravine, the trail climbs toward the west, crosses side drainages and parallels the primary stream until it enters a cove of Harsha Lake.

Angling northward, the trail roller-coasters through the forest, crossing five creek beds, before emerging onto a Park road. The clearing above the road offers a broad view of Harsha Lake. The path crosses the road, descends a long stairway and curves to the right, heading eastward through the lakeside forest. After crossing several more drainages, the trail enters a clearing above East Fork's Beach Area which offers another sweeping view of the Reservoir.

Re-entering the forest, the route crosses the Beach access road, skirts a picnic area, dips through a ravine and arrives at a junction where a white-blazed trail leads southward to Overnight Area #1. Bear right onto this path, cross another roadway and hike ¼ mile through open woods to the campsite.

Continue southward past the Overnight Area and you will soon intersect the **Backcountry Trail (BCT)**, blazed with green. Turn right (west) for a short hike back to the Main Trailhead area. This last segment crosses through open woodland, curves past a small pond and emerges onto the south entrance road, just across from the Trailhead parking area. Your hike has totalled 5 miles.

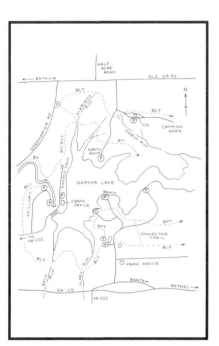

The Main Trailhead

**EAST FORK STATE PARK
(WESTERN SECTION)**

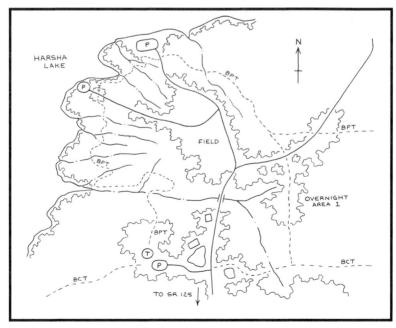

BACKPACK / BACK-COUNTRY LOOP

Backcountry Trail (Campground Office to Saddle Dam); 12.0 miles round-trip. This long day hike begins at the parking lot adjacent to the Campground Office (CO). As mentioned above, the **Backcountry Trail** is also open to horseback riders and sections of the route, especially near stream crossings, can be nearly impassable after periods of wet weather. Trail conditions are best in mid winter but waterproof hiking boots are advised in all seasons.

From the lot, cross the road and access the **Backcountry Trail (BCT)** via a short spur path (see map). Turn left (west) paralleling the road and then crossing it. Cutting through a woodland, the trail dips through the upper reaches of Cabin Run, crosses a boggy meadow and emerges along the road to East Fork's North Boat Ramp. The path follows the road for about ¼ mile, crosses it and heads westward along the edge of a woodland. A short distance in from the road, the route turns north along an abandoned lane and then cuts back to the west. You will soon pass Overnight Area #4.

Beyond the campsite, the trail crosses upper drainages of Slabcamp Run, cuts through a parking lot on Greenbrier Road and then angles to the south, descending into Slabcamp Hollow. Within this ravine the **Backcountry Trail** intersects the Buckeye Trail (BT). Bear right, following the combined **BCT/BT** route for a gradual 2 mile ascent to the Saddle Dam. From the top of the Dam, you are treated to spectacular views of Harsha Lake, to the east, and the East Fork Valley, to the west. A large number of turkey vultures roost along the Dam from March to October; they sun themselves on the rock wall during the morning hours and soar effortlessly above the valley at mid day. The deep waters along the Saddle Dam attract migrant loons, grebes and diving ducks during spring and fall.

After rest and nourishment atop the Dam, return to the Campground lot via the same route for a roundtrip hike of 12.0 miles.

Directions:

The Main Trailhead (T) lot is south of the reservoir. From Bethel, Ohio, drive west on S.R. 125 for 3.7 miles and angle to the right on Bantam Road. Proceed through the small community and turn right (north) on the entry road for East Fork State Park. Continue approximately ½ mile and watch for the parking area entrance, on your left (just south of a marsh-lined pond).

The Campground Lot is north of the reservoir. From Batavia, follow S.R. 32 eastward for about 4 miles and exit onto Half Acre Road. Drive south for 1 mile and turn left (east) on Old S.R. 32. Watch for the East Fork entrance on your right. Approximately .4 mile in from the entrance, turn left onto the Campground access road and proceed to the large lot next to the check-in office.

The East Fork Valley

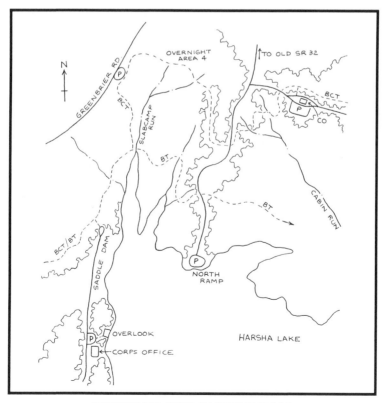

ROUTE TO THE SADDLE DAM

43 ROCKY FORK STATE PARK

Distance: 3.5 miles
Terrain: rolling; few steep areas

Winding eastward toward the Appalachian Front, the Rocky Fork Valley yields a picturesque setting for one of our more popular State Parks. Its 2080 acre reservoir, created for flood control in the early 1950s, is heavily used by boaters and fishermen.

While the Park also encompasses almost 1400 acres of land, most of this acreage is stretched along the shoreline of the lake. As a result, extensive hiking trails are not available at Rocky Fork. Nevertheless, the following route combines respectable distance with some interesting topography.

Trail Route:

Park in the large lot off North Shore Road, adjacent to the reservoir's northwest inlet (see map). Walk back to the road and turn right (east), crossing the inlet channel.

Just across the bridge the trailhead for the **Paw Paw (A)** and **Redbud (B) Trails** will be noted on your right. Cross the footbridge, ascend a few stairs and continue straight ahead at the trail intersection. The .75 mile **Paw Paw** loop winds along the higher/drier ground of this mini-peninsula and offers changing views of the lake. Several small spur trails, presumably created by deer or bank fishermen, lead off to the right and descend to the floodplain of the reservoir.

Unless you're fond of thickets, mosquitos and muck, bypass the .5 mile **Redbud Trail** and stay on higher ground, looping back to the entry bridge. Exit the woodland and turn right along North Shore Road. Walk eastward for approximately 100 yards and find the trailhead for the **Deer Loop Trail (C)** on the north side of the road, just beyond the maintenance area. While the sign indicates a 1 mile loop, the distance is probably closer to 1.5 miles. Ascend the hillside and curve to the right through the grassy field. Enter the woods and wind northward, crossing several shallow drainages.

The trail eventually curves to the west, dips through a ravine and then enters a clearing. Knifing back into the forest, the trail hugs the edge of a steep cliff where the terrain plummets into the Rocky Fork basin. Extensive views unfold during the colder months and wildlife watchers may want to stop along the ridge to peruse the wetlands below.

After winding along the clifftop for approximately 1/3 mile, the trail cuts away from the edge and rollercoasters across several side ravines, finally emerging at the west end of the hillside meadow. Descend to the North Shore Road and walk back to the parking area, completing a hike of approximately 3.5 miles.

Directions:

Follow S.R. 124 south and east from Hillsboro. Drive approximately 3 miles and turn left (east) on North Shore Road. Pass the airport and watch for the State Park entrance, on your right. Park in the large lot just south of the ranger booth (see map).

The Northwest Inlet

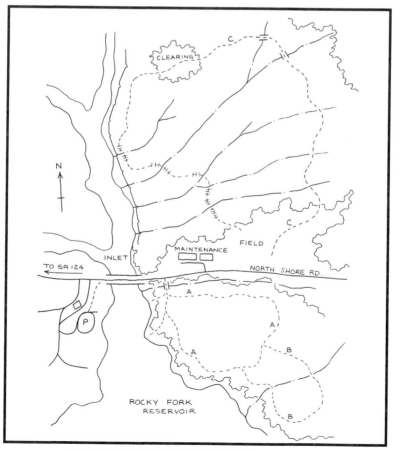

TRAILS OF ROCKY FORK STATE PARK

44 PAINT CREEK STATE PARK

Distance: Day hikes of 3.0 and 3.5 miles
Terrain: rolling; some hilly areas with moderate grades

Originating west of London, Ohio, Paint Creek flows south and eastward for 97 miles before entering the Scioto River at Chillicothe. Drawing from a watershed of 1143 square miles, this stream and its major tributary, Rattlesnake Creek, carved a deep gorge through the Silurian bedrock of southern Ohio. Now drowned by a flood-control reservoir, the chasm's former grandeur is still evident below the dam, where steep walls of shale, limestone and dolomite rise above the Creek.

The 1200 acre reservoir, completed in 1974, is now surrounded by 9000 acres of State Park land. Access to this extensive preserve is off Rapid Forge Road, east of the lake, or via S.R. 753, north of Rainsboro. The following day hikes are suggested.

Trail Routes:

Little Pond Trail/Bridal Path Loop (3.0 mile hike). This hike begins at a parking lot just north of the Dam. Enter the forest and bear left at the trail intersection. You will soon cross a stream that flows through a "hanging valley," formed by the collapse of a limestone cave.

Emerging from the woods, turn left and descend along an open meadow. Views of the reservoir and of the "Appalachian Front" unfold to the south. At the bottom of the slope, short side trails lead down to the water's edge.

Loop around to the north, following a wide bridal path (see map). At the next intersection, angle to the left and climb onto the ridge for expansive views of the Paint Creek region. Follow the trail northward as it winds higher along the ridge, crossing fields and open woodlands. The route eventually curves to the east and begins a gradual descent from the ridge. Pass a cutoff to a camping area, on your left, and at the bottom of the slope, angle to the right, crossing a broad meadow with scattered wildlife plantings. The faint trail leads to the south and runs along the eastern side of a shrub-line.

Continue southward to the lake, backtracking along your earlier route. Loop to the north, bypass the entry trail and snake along the shoreline of Little Pond. Winding in and out of numerous coves, the trail crosses several feeder streams and eventually returns to the parking area.

*Bridge
across the
"hanging valley"*

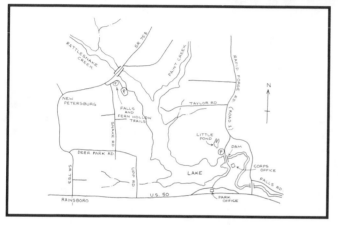

**PAINT CREEK
STATE PARK**

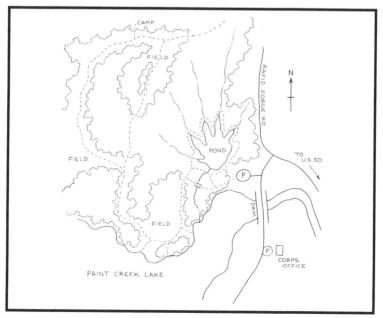

LITTLE POND TRAIL / BRIDAL PATH LOOP

117

Falls Trail/Fern Hollow Loop (3.5 mile hike). A combined hike along the **Falls Trail** and **Fern Hollow Trail** yields a pleasant hike above the Rattlesnake inlet of Paint Creek Reservoir. Park in the small lot that services the **Falls Trail**, just off the road to the Rattlesnake boat ramp (see map).

Hike southward, ascending into an open woodland and soon winding along the edge of the Reservoir's basin. The trail is faint in some areas and, to date, has not been blazed. After hiking about .5 mile, follow the trail as it dips below the rocky outcrops that cap the edge of the basin. Now covered by moss, the Silurian dolomite has been exposed by continued erosion along the wall of Rattlesnake gorge.

Climbing back onto the plateau, the trail leads across a feeder stream and soon intersects a side trail to the Falls overlook. Take this short walk to the Falls, where a rocky prominance offers a splendid view of the cascade.

Return to the **Falls Trail** and turn left (south). Crossing a second stream, the trail leads upward into the drier forest. A short hike through this woodland brings you to the intersection with the 1.5 mile **Fern Hollow Loop.**

Turn left, descending via a series of wooden stairs. Cross to the **Fern Hollow** trailhead (see map) and begin an easy stroll along a wide, level path that leads southward, passing between the reservoir and the steep gorge wall. Slump blocks of dolo-mite, having broken from the cliffs, rest along the trail. At Fern Hollow, the trail curves to the west and then takes a sharp turn to the left, leaving the old roadbed (watch for the trail marker). Wind down to the stream bed where clumps of scouring rush adorn the winding channel. Christmas ferns are abundant in this moist ravine.

The trail leads upstream and eventually turns to the north, ascending to higher terrain. This section of the route is somewhat difficult to follow until it levels out and cuts through a dense briar patch. You will soon emerge onto a meadow and intersect the old roadbed. Turn left, hike about 50 yards and then turn right onto a trail that skirts the edge of the meadow (see map). Deer are often encountered in this area, especially at dawn or dusk. A short hike through the forest brings you back to the intersection with the **Falls Trail**. Bear left and retrace the one mile route to the parking lot.

Directions:

Paint Creek State Park is located north of U.S. 50, approximately 12 miles east of Hillsboro. The Rattlesnake inlet area is just east of S.R. 753, 4.6 miles north of Rainsboro. The Dam area, including the trailhead lot for the Little Pond Trail, is reached via Rapid Forge Road (Park Road #1) which runs north from U.S. 50, approximately 13 miles east of Hillsboro (3 miles east of Rainsboro).

The Rattlesnake Inlet

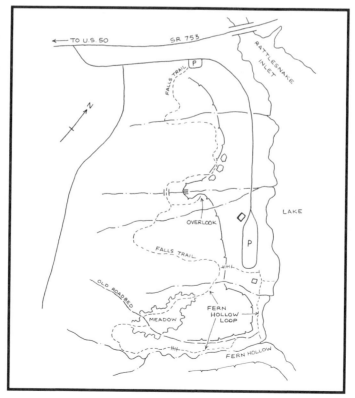

FALLS TRAIL / FERN HOLLOW

45 FORT HILL STATE MEMORIAL

Distance: 5.0 miles
Terrain: hilly; steep areas

Perched atop a spur ridge of the Appalachian Plateau, a prehistoric, ceremonial "fort" is the centerpiece of the Fort Hill State Memorial. The fort is enclosed by a 1.6 mile earthen/rock wall, now reclaimed by vegetation, which was constructed by the Hopewell Indians. These "mound-builders" occupied the area from 200 B.C. to 300 A.D.

The State Memorial, managed by the Ohio Historical Society, protects the fort and offers superb hiking through scenic terrain. Eleven miles of trails wind through the preserve and provide access to its varied habitat and cultural artifacts. A museum (M), open from March to October, educates the visitor regarding the natural history of the area.

I recommend a winter visit to Fort Hill. The summer crowds are gone, vistas are broader, insects are hibernating, footing is better and wildlife is more conspicuous. White-tailed deer and ruffed grouse are almost certain to be seen on a crisp winter day. Huge icicles adorn the rock walls of Baker Fork Gorge and a blanket of snow adds to the beauty of this peaceful retreat.

Trail Route:

The following 5.0 mile hike takes you through the Baker Fork Gorge and across the Hopewell fortress. From the east end of the parking lot, follow the **Gorge Trail (GT)** and **Deer Trail (DT)** northwestward along a side stream. This is also a section of the **Buckeye Trail (BT)**. The route curves to the left and soon parallels Baker Fork Creek, a major tributary of Ohio Brush Creek.

As the stream curves to the north, the trail angles southwestward and crosses a low ridge. Descending to the creek again, you begin a 1.5 mile journey through Baker Fork Gorge. Outcroppings of Silurian dolomite line the stream and numerous tree trunks, uprooted by cliffside erosion, are strewn across the gorge walls. The dead timber attracts the many woodpeckers that inhabit the preserve.

After a short distance you will arrive at a trail intersection (see map). The **Deer Trail** and **Buckeye Trail** turn right (west) and cross Baker Fork Creek. Turn left and follow the **Gorge Trail** as it ascends into the forest, passes an old cabin (C) and then descends into the gorge again. Continuing southward you will wind across, under, over and through the exposed dolomite cliffs. Natural bridges (NB), formed by water erosion, will be noted across the stream (see map).

The **Deer** and **Buckeye Trails** rejoin the **Gorge Trail** and all three continue southward for another .5 mile. They then angle to the east, ascending into the forest along a side stream. Crossing the stream, the path makes a broad switchback and ascends onto a low ridge. At the next intersection the **Buckeye Trail** turns to the south; follow the **Gorge Trail** and **Deer Trail** as they continue a gentle climb to the north. Another .25 mile brings you to a fork in the trail where the **Deer Trail** splits to the right. Bear left onto the **Gorge Trail** and begin a moderately steep climb toward the hilltop fortress. Leveling out along a terrace, the **Gorge Trail** merges with the south arm of the **Fort Trail**.

Angle back to the left and follow the **Fort Trail** as it winds around the side of the ridge. You are walking along the western edge of the Appalachian Plateau and expansive views unfold to the south and west. East Hill (EH) rises to the southeast while Jarnigan Knob (JK) and Reeds Hill (RH) dominate the western view. The south wall of the Hopewell Fortress, notched by erosion, stretches atop the ridge, to your right.

At the west end of the loop the trail angles eastward and a short but steep climb brings you into the ancient fort and onto the flat top of Fort Hill. The trail parallels the north wall of the fort. You will note

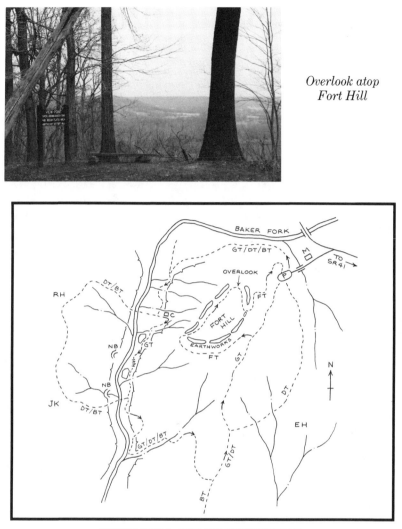

Overlook atop Fort Hill

FORT HILL STATE MEMORIAL

that the mounds were constructed with earth and with rock. The latter is Berea sandstone, which dates from the Mississippian Period. This resistant rock caps Fort Hill and the other "knobs" that rise above the Baker Fork valley. An overlook, at the north end of the fort, provides a spectacular view of the valley as it stretches to the northeast of Fort Hill. Standing at an elevation of almost 1300 feet, you are 423 feet above the level of the stream.

After taking in the view, cross through the south wall of the fort and descend to the parking area via the north arm of the **Fort Trail** loop (see map).

Directions:

Fort Hill State Memorial lies west of S.R. 41, 10.5 miles southwest of Bainbridge, Ohio. From Hillsboro, follow U.S. 50 east for 10 miles. Turn right (south) on S.R. 753 and drive 7 miles, knifing into the edge of the Appalachian Plateau. Turn right (south) on S.R. 41, proceed .5 mile and turn right onto the Fort Hill entry road.

46 ADAMS LAKE PRAIRIE STATE NATURE PRESERVE

Distance: 1-1.5 miles
Terrain: hilly; moderate grades

The xeric prairie remnants of Adams County are thought to be "offspring" from larger grasslands that spread across the region some 5000 years ago. Thin, unglaciated soil, unable to support deciduous forest, favored the evolution of "dry prairies." These unique areas, characterized by shortgrass species, wildflowers and cedar groves, still dot the rocky hillsides where constant erosion retards the invasion of surrounding woodlands.

Along the margin of these prairie openings, accumulation of leaves and other deciduous "waste" enriches the soil and permits the oaks, hickories and locust trees to slowly reclaim the land. If left undisturbed, these small grasslands will eventually succumb to expansion of the forest. Even today, the visitor will find red cedar, post oak, black locust, shrubby St. John's-wort, white oak and shingle oak extending their domain into the prairie.

Adams Lake Prairie State Nature Preserve, located within Adams Lake State Park, protects one of the larger xeric prairies in southern Ohio. Dedicated in May, 1973, the 22 acre site harbors a vast array of plant life. Typical prairie species include prairie dock, flowering spurge, black-eyed Susan, butterfly weed, hoary puccoon, pale-spike lobelia, coneflowers, rose-pink, shooting-star and prairie rose. Dominant grasses are little blue stem and side-oats gramma.

Trail Route:
The trail through this small but fasci-

nating preserve starts south of the Park's roadway, .4 mile in from S.R. 41 and across from a small parking lot. A short distance in from the road, the trail forks. Bear left onto the **Post Oak Trail (A)** and wind eastward through the forest, crossing several drainage channels. The trail curves to the south and climbs steadily up the hillside. Near the top of the ridge, the trail cuts back to the west and eventually emerges from the oak-hickory forest into the xeric prairie opening.

Bear left onto the **Prairie Dock Trail (B)**. Boardwalks elevate the trail above drainages and serve to minimize visitor impact on this fragile environment. The trail follows the margin of the prairie but loops inward enough to provide a close look at the numerous plant species. Watch for ant hills along the trail, the handiwork of red, "Allegheny mountain ants."

Completing the prairie loop, turn left for a short walk to the parking area or retrace your route along the **Post Oak Trail** to add another .5 mile to your hike.

Directions:
Adams Lake State Park and its Prairie Preserve are located approximately 1 mile northeast of West Union on the west side of S.R. 41. Park in the small lot near the west end of the lake, .4 mile in from the entrance. The Nature Preserve stretches south from the road (see map).

A typical scene on the xeric prairie

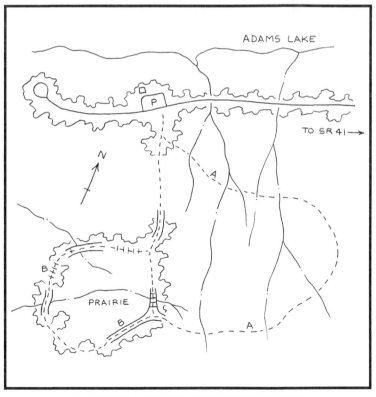

ADAMS LAKE NATURE PRESERVE

47 EDGE OF APPALACHIA/BUZZARDROOST ROCK

Distance: 4 miles roundtrip
Terrain: hilly; steep climbs

Geologists and physiographers tend to ignore State and National boundaries, preferring to view each continent as a composite of geologic provinces. Ohio straddles two of these provinces; the northwestern 60% of our State lies in the Central Lowlands of North America while the southeastern 40% is part of the Appalachian Plateau. The latter is a broad, uplifted area of horizontal sediments, stretching from the Catskills of New York to northern Alabama. A third province, the Interior Low Plateau, pokes into Adams County, in south-central Ohio.

The western edge of the Appalachian Plateau has been obscured by glacial erosion in northern Ohio. However, from the Circleville area southward, this escarpment stands out as a prominent ridge, rising 300-500 feet above the lowlands to the west. Such transition zones, harboring a tremendous diversity of habitat, yield natural wonderlands for the biologist.

The Cincinnati Museum of Natural History, in concert with the Nature Conservancy, has established a twelve-mile chain of nature preserves along this "Edge of Appalachia," paralleling the course of Ohio Brush Creek, in Adams County. The area is characterized by rugged cliffs, xeric prairies, cedar groves and peri-glacial relic communities. The latter include stands of northern white cedar and scattered clumps of sullivantia. Six species of orchid grace the Edge and the region's diverse fauna include two endangered species, the green salamander and the eastern woodrat.

Trail Route:

Perhaps the best hiking trail in the Edge of Appalachia Preserves is the 2.0 mile climb to Buzzardroost Rock from a small parking lot on Weaver Road (see Directions). The trail to this National Natural Landmark leaves the west end of the graveled lot and angles downhill, crossing S.R. 125. It continues down to a scenic sidestream which flows westward into Ohio Brush Creek. Crossing the stream via a footbridge, the trail winds up the opposite slope, cutting through an open cedar glade.

Climbing gradually higher and southward, the trail enters a dense woodland and swings to the west of a higher ridge. Rugged cliffs of dolomite soon appear above you on the left, resembling a medieval fortress. Further along, giant slump blocks, having broken from the upper cliffs, rest along the trail. About one mile from the parking lot the trail turns eastward and climbs the steep ridge via a series of switchbacks. At the crest of the ridge the route leads southward again, dipping through a ravine.

Once past the ravine, watch for a sign that directs you to the right. This last section of the trail winds to the southwest, running atop a side-ridge that terminates at Buzzardroost Rock. Deep ravines flank the ridge and expansive views of the Ohio Brush Creek Valley soon unfold to the west. From the Buzzardroost overlook, almost 500 feet above the valley floor, spectacular views reward your effort. Farms dot the Valley and Ohio Route 125 curves away to the northwest. The gorge to the southeast of the overlook is especially scenic.

After a bit of rest and inspiration at the Rock, return to the parking area via the same route for a total hike of 4 miles.

Directions:

Follow S.R. 125 east from West Union. Six miles from the town square you will cross Ohio Brush Creek. Twenty yards beyond the Creek, turn left onto a narrow lane (Weaver Road) and follow it for .9 miles to a small parking area, on your right. This hike is especially popular on October weekends and the limited parking space can pose a problem. If possible, plan a weekday or "off-season" visit.

The overlook is a National Natural Landmark.

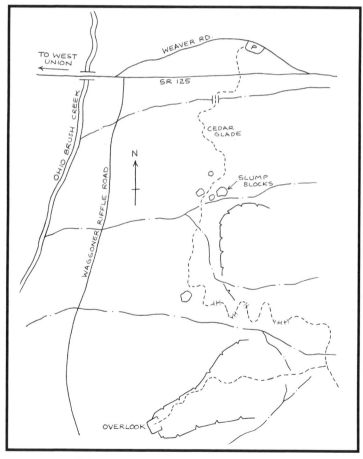

TRAIL TO BUZZARDSROOST ROCK

48 SHAWNEE STATE FOREST

Distance: Day hikes of 10.6 and 12.0 miles
Terrain: hilly; steep areas

Shawnee State Forest, sprawling across 60,000 acres, represents the largest unbroken expanse of forest in Ohio. Often called the "Little Smokies," the numerous ridges of Shawnee have been carved from the Appalachian Plateau by the erosive power of its many streams. Ridgetops average 1100 feet in elevation while valley floors are 750 to 800 feet above sea level.

Home to Shawnee State Park, the Forest offers a wide diversity of recreation, including over 60 miles of hiking trails and 70 miles of bridal paths. A 42.8 mile **Backpack Trail** winds through the forest and a 10.5 mile side loop cuts through Shawnee's Wilderness Preserve. While there are numerous graveled "pull-offs" along the Forest roads, safe and reliable parking is limited to the Main Backpack Lot, north of Turkey Creek Lake, and at Camp Oyo, on the north side of S.R. 125 and 2 miles east of the Lake (see map).

Since the primary **Backpack Trail** is too long for a day hike, I recommend the following routes. These, too, are quite long and should be undertaken only by fit and experienced hikers. The hilly terrain makes for strenuous hiking and the distances will seem longer than those stated below.

Trail Routes:
A. Main Backpack Lot to Copperhead Fire Tower (roundtrip distance of 10.6 miles). From the Backpack Lot, north of Turkey Creek Lake, cross S.R. 125 and ascend from the roadway via a short earthen stairway. The trail soon forks with the main **Backpack Trail (BPT)**, blazed in red-orange, going left and a **Connecting Trail (CT)** to Camp Oyo, blazed in white, going right. Turn left and follow the **Backpack Trail** as it descends through Hoosler Hollow and then leads onto the opposite ridge. The trail heads north along the ridge, descends to a creek bed and follows one branch of the stream for a gradual one-mile climb to Forest Road #6.

Turn right and hike eastward along Road #6 to the Copperhead Fire Tower, a distance of 2.3 miles. Forest Road #6 is a narrow, gravel road that follows the crest of the ridge and offers several excellent views along the way. Except on warm weather weekends, vehicle traffic is sparce and the road is trail-like in nature.

The Copperhead Fire Tower sits at an elevation of 1220 feet, 430 feet higher than the trailhead parking lot. Unfortunately, the tower is currently closed to the public; however, the clearing at its base still affords a broad view to the south. Views to the north are best achieved from the Copperhead Ridge Overlook, just west of the tower along Forest Road #6.

After a ridgetop picnic, return to the Backpack Lot via the same route for a roundtrip hike of 10.6 miles.

A view to the north from Road 6

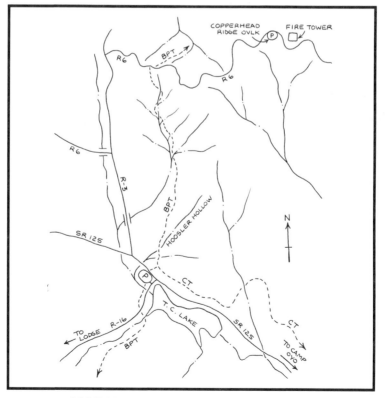

MAIN TRAILHEAD TO FIRE TOWER

B. Camp Oyo to Copperhead Fire Tower (roundtrip distance of 12.0 miles). Access to this hike is via the parking lot at Camp Oyo, north of S.R. 125 and 2 miles east of Turkey Creek Lake. From the lot, walk north along Forest Road #1 for approximately 1/3 mile. Turn right onto the Shawnee **Backpack Trail (BPT)** which crosses the road and begins a one-mile ascent of the ridge to the east. Near the crest of the ridge, turn left onto the **Silver Arrow Trail (SAT)** which leads northward along the ridgetop.

A long, mostly level hike takes you across Forest Road #1 and then angles to the northwest. One mile beyond the Road the **Silver Arrow Trail** again crosses the **Backpack Trail**, veers westward and intercepts the north end of the **Rock Lick Bridal Path (RLB).** Exit onto Forest Road #6 and turn left for a .5 mile walk to the Copperhead Fire Tower. See the preceding trail narrative for discussion of the Tower area. Descend via the same route for a roundtrip hike of 12.0 miles.

Directions:

Shawnee State Forest and State Park are located along S.R. 125, approximately 6 miles northwest of the U.S. 52/S.R. 125 junction. The main Backpack Lot is just north of Turkey Creek Lake, off Forest Road #16. Camp Oyo is north of S.R. 125, about 2 miles east of the Lake.

Autumn in the forest

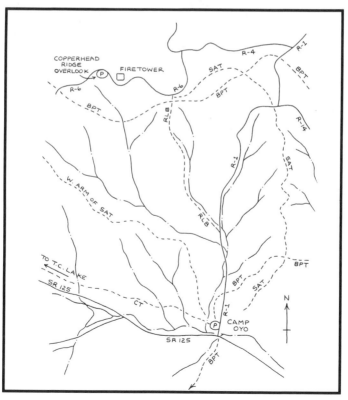

CAMP OYO TO FIRE TOWER

VI. HIKING AREAS OF SOUTHEAST OHIO

49. Stage's Pond State Nature Preserve

50. Shallenberger State Nature Preserve

51. Dysart Woods

52. Rockbridge State Nature Preserve

53. Wildcat Hollow

54. Hocking State Park

55. Conkles Hollow State Nature Preserve

56. Cantwell Cliffs

57. Great Seal State Park

58. Tar Hollow State Forest

59. Lake Hope State Park

60. Zaleski State Forest

61. Strouds Run State Park

62. Scioto Trail State Park

63. Lake Katharine State Nature Preserve

64. Lake Vesuvius Recreation Area

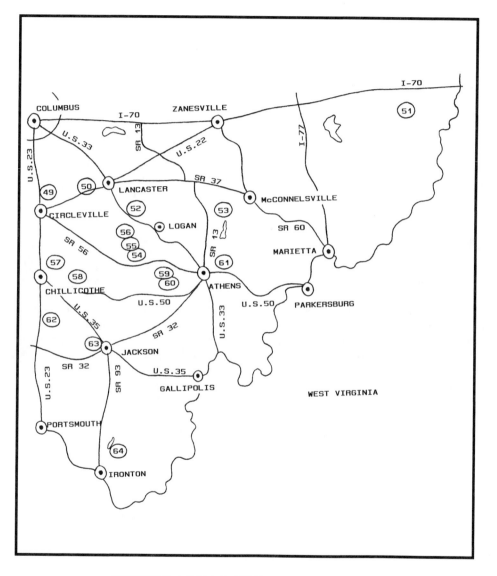

HIKING AREAS OF SOUTHEAST OHIO

49 STAGE'S POND STATE NATURE PRESERVE

Distance: 3.0 miles
Terrain: rolling

The topography of western and northern Ohio was greatly altered by the Pleistocene glaciers. Remnants of their activity persist across the region today. Stage's Pond, four miles north of Circleville, provides an excellent example.

As the Wisconsin ice sheet retreated into Canada, some 15,000 years ago, a massive slab of ice broke from its undersurface and was embedded in the soft glacial till of central Ohio. With continued warming of the earth's climate, the ice melted and a 64 acre depression was left in its place. Filled by drainage from adjacent uplands, the basin became a "kettle lake" which has since diminished in size as silt and vegetation have reclaimed its shallows. The present day 30-acre pond lies at the northern end of the basin; shallow sloughs and marshes extend across the depression to the south.

Through the combined efforts of the Pickaway County Garden Club, the Nature Conservancy and the Ohio Department of Natural Resources, this kettle lake is now protected within the 178-acre Stage's Pond State Nature Preserve, dedicated in August, 1974. A three mile hike through the Preserve takes you across the kettle lake basin and through upland forest that borders the wetland.

Trail Route:

From the parking area, walk to the west and proceed out to the Bird Blind for an overview of the pond's basin. The extensive marshland before you fills with migrant waterfowl during spring and fall. A plaque in the observation hut illustrates the many species that frequent the Preserve.

Return to the **Moraine Trail (A)** and hike northward. More views of the basin unfold on your left. Dip through a shallow ravine and continue northward along a stream, slowly climbing into the forest.

Bear left onto the **Kettle Lake Trail (B)** and pass the cutoff to the **Multiflora Trail (C)**, on your right. Wind downhill into the basin and hike .5 mile across open marshland to Stage's Pond. The trail continues along the western shore of the lake, ending at Ward Road. Backtrack across the basin, watching for ring-necked pheasants that often forage along the trail.

Ascend to higher ground and bear left onto the **Multiflora Trail (C)** which winds along the edge of this low ridge. Views of the basin and of Stage's Pond are extensive during the colder months. At the intersection with the **Moraine Trail (A)**, turn left and proceed to the **White Oak Trail (D)**, a .7 mile loop through the upland forest. Complete the circuit and return to the parking lot via the **Moraine Trail.**

Directions:

From Circleville, drive north on U.S. 23 for 4 miles. Turn right (east) on Hagerty Road. Proceed 1.6 miles to the Preserve, on your left. The entrance is .5 mile beyond Ward Road.

Late summer at the pond

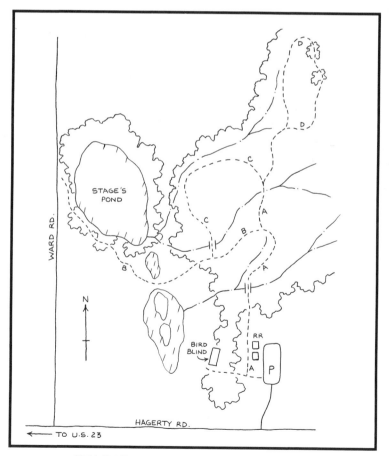

STAGE'S POND NATURE PRESERVE

50 SHALLENBERGER STATE NATURE PRESERVE

Distance: 2.0 miles
Terrain: hilly; steep areas

Fifteen thousand years ago, the Wisconsin Ice Sheet plowed into the western edge of the Appalachian Plateau, grinding away surface rock and dumping glacial till across the flattened landscape. In some areas, the rock surface was high enough to escape the erosive force of the ice. As the climate warmed and the glacier retreated into Canada, water erosion sculpted the countryside and the islands of unglaciated rock, more resistant than the surrounding till, protected underlying layers of sediment. As a result, a chain of "knobs" now stretch from north to south along the western margin of the Appalachian Plateau.

Further weathering of these rocky islands produced a thin, nutrient-poor soil atop the knobs. Chestnut oak and mountain laurel, tolerant of such conditions, now thrive on the windswept summits. Walking fern, ebony spleen-wort and polypody fern cling to the sandstone walls while red oaks, maples, ash and hickory grow on the lower, glaciated slopes.

Shallenberger State Nature Preserve, an 88 acre refuge west of Lancaster, protects two of these knobs. Dedicated in May, 1973, the preserve was originally donated to Fairfield County by Jay M. Shallenberger. Transferred to the State of Ohio, it is now managed by the Ohio Department of Natural Resources. The following route yields a 2.0 mile hike and takes the visitor atop the Preserve's sandstone knobs.

Trail Route:
From the parking lot, hike eastward into the forest. Bear right at the fork in the trail, gradually ascending along the south side of Allen Knob. At the next intersection, angle to the left and begin a short but steep climb **(A)** to the knob's summit (elevation 1140 feet). A sinkhole marks the center of this isolated plateau and the rocky margins of the knob harbor one of the more concentrated stands of mountain laurel in Ohio. From its natural overlooks, Allen Knob yields sweeping views of the rolling farmlands west of Lancaster. The Hunter Run Valley, north of the knob, lies 270 feet below the summit.

Retrace your route to the base of Allen Knob and turn left, descending into a side ravine of Hunter Run. This section can be treacherous after periods of rain. Cross the creek and follow the **Arrowhead Trail (B)** as it ascends along the north side of Ruble Knob. Near the east end of the Preserve, the trail forks. Bear right and climb to the top of Ruble Knob, an elevation of 1090 feet.

Descend to the base and bear right onto the **Honeysuckle Trail (C)**. Winding northward and then curving to the west, this trail crosses several drainages. Nearing the primary stream the route angles to the south for a short distance and then turns west, crossing the creek via a wooden bridge.

Climb westward and bear right at the next intersection, following the **Honeysuckle Trail** as it circles around the base of Allen Knob. After curving around the west end of the Knob a set of stairs brings you down to the entry trail. Turn right for a short walk back to the parking lot.

Directions:
From U.S. 33 in Lancaster, turn west onto U.S. 22. Drive 3.2 miles and turn right (north) on Becks Knob Road. Proceed .2 mile to the Preserve, on your right.

Mountain laurel atop Allen Knob

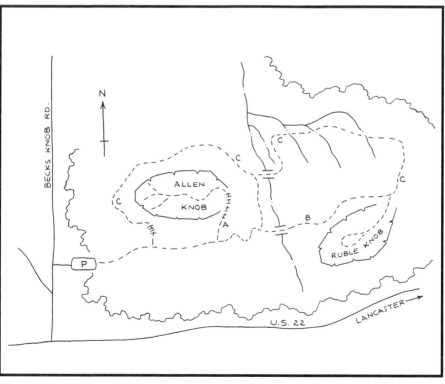

SHALLENBERGER PRESERVE

51 DYSART WOODS

Distance: 2.0 miles
Terrain: hilly; moderate grades

Driving across the rolling countryside of Belmont County, the landscape is dominated by open grasslands, cultivated fields, cattle ranches and reclaimed strip mines. Once cloaked by a vast hardwood forest, this section of the Appalachian Plateau has witnessed a continual loss of woodland ever since white settlers first arrived during the early 19th Century. Amidst such widespread forest destruction, one would not expect to find what is perhaps Ohio's most renowned stand of virgin timber.

Dysart Woods, a 50 acre tract of uncut hardwood forest, has somehow survived the onslaught of the axe and plow. Secluded within two deep ravines, approximately 4 miles southeast of Belmont, the Woods were likely an inconvenient target for the loggers. The virgin timber is now protected within the Dysart Woods Laboratory of Ohio University and was designated a National Natural Landmark in 1967.

Characterized by huge specimens of beech, oak, hickory, maple, tulip poplar and ash, the Preserve is accessed by a 2-mile, double-loop trail, blazed with painted posts. The two stands of virgin hardwood are separated by a ridge of dense, immature forest which is bisected by Township Road 194.

Trail Route:

From the parking area on Township Road 194, follow the **Blue Trail (B)** which leads eastward into the forest. Winding into a deep ravine, the immature woodland yields to the more open domain of the hardwood giants. Cross the creek and turn right. An elongated loop leads southward across the east wall of the ravine.

Completing the loop, continue northward on the **Blue Trail** which heads upstream and begins a steady climb to the crest of the ridge. Cross the road and descend into the next ravine via the **Red Trail (R)**. Once again, the young, cluttered forest on the upper slopes gives way to virgin timber in the deep ravine. Some of the ancient trees have fallen across the trail and a bit of log-hopping may be necessary along the way. Such fallen timber attracts the numerous woodpeckers that noisily haunt the forest and hollowed trunks offer shelter for squirrels, chipmunks and raccoons. Cavities within the upright giants are used by wood ducks which may whistle through the trees as you approach.

At the bottom of the ravine, the **Red Trail** crosses two streams and leads onto the western slope. A short climb takes you past a huge tulip poplar (T), thought to be the largest of its species in Ohio. Winding back into the ravine, the trail re-crosses the primary stream and begins a long, steady ascent to the parking area. Watch for American woodcocks that inhabit the moist borders of the forest, using nearby meadows for their spectacular mating flights in early spring.

Directions:

From I-70, take Exit #208 and head south on S.R. 149. Drive 2.5 miles, turn left on S.R. 147 and wind through the town of Belmont. Continue toward the southeast on S.R. 147 for another 4 miles and turn right at the sign for Dysart Woods Laboratory. Bear right onto Township Road 194 and proceed approximately .75 mile to the parking lot, on your left.

*One of many
giants along
the trail*

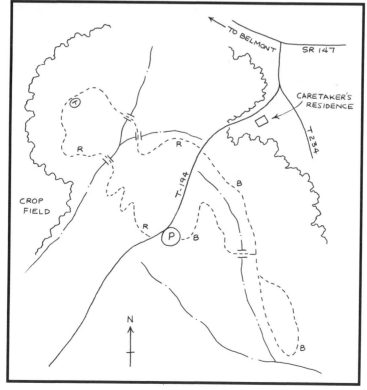

DYSART WOODS

52 ROCKBRIDGE STATE NATURE PRESERVE

Distance: 1.75 miles
Terrain: hilly; steep areas

Tucked away above the west bank of the Hocking River, Rockbridge State Nature Preserve is a little known and sparsely utilized area. Yet, its natural arch (the largest in Ohio) and adjacent recessed cave have provided shelter and inspiration for man since prehistoric time.

Trail Route:

A 1.75 mile trail winds through the Preserve, crossing its varied habitats. From the parking area, the trail makes a beeline to the northeast, leading across the rolling farmlands of Hocking County. Pastures stretch to the north while a cornfield spreads southward from the trail. A long, steady climb brings you to the top of a ridge and yields a broad view to the west.

Descending a short distance, the trail forks. Turn left, following the **Natural Bridge Trail (A)**. This path leads northward along the west wall of a deep ravine where a recovering woodland is characterized by shrubs, patches of dogwood and open stands of Virginia pine. Views of the Hocking River valley unfold to the northeast.

Angling to the right, the trail winds into the ravine, enters the mature forest and parallels the stream. After crossing the primary channel, a short walk brings you to the Natural Bridge, on your left. The arch, composed of resistant Blackhand sandstone (Mississippian age), formed as erosional forces along a fracture eventually separated the span from the rest of the ledge. A 50-foot waterfall now plunges through the gap as the stream makes its way to the Hocking River. Behind the falls, a recessed cave has formed as softer bedrock has worn away beneath the Blackhand sandstone.

For your return trip, follow the **Beech Ridge Trail (B)** which ascends into the higher, drier forest, south of the Natural Bridge. This second-growth woodland is characterized by oak, hickory and beech trees, providing food and shelter for white-tailed deer, ruffed grouse, gray fox, wild turkey and other forest creatures. From late autumn through early spring, sweeping views of the Hocking Valley reward your effort. A variety of wildflowers, including dwarf iris and Indian pipe, carpet the forest floor during the warmer months.

After a short course along the ridge, the trail veers to the right, descends into the ravine, crosses the stream and leads up through the shrub/pine community on the west wall. Continue straight ahead at the trail intersection and begin the long descent to the parking area.

Directions:

Rockbridge State Nature Preserve is located east of U.S. 33, approximately 5 miles northwest of Logan. From the junction of S.R. 180 and U.S. 33, proceed north on 33 for ½ mile. Turn right (east) onto Township Road 124 which immediately deadends into Township Road 503 (also called Dalton Road). Turn right and follow this road as it parallels U.S. 33 a short distance and then curves to the east. The parking lot for the Rockbridge Preserve will be .8 mile on your left.

Ohio's largest natural bridge

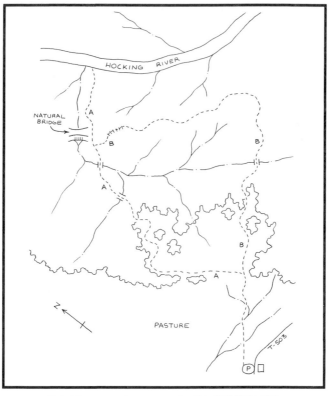

ROCKBRIDGE NATURE PRESERVE

139

53 WILDCAT HOLLOW

Distance: 5 miles
Terrain: hilly; moderate grades

Wildcat Hollow is a primitive weapons hunting area within Wayne National Forest, just northeast of Burr Oak State Park. Drained by tributaries of Sunday Creek, the wooded ridges are typical of the Appalachian Plateau. Oak-hickory forest dominates on dry, sunny slopes while pockets of maple, beech and ash cluster along the moist ravines. Stands of pine are scattered through the forest and ridgetop clearings enrich the natural diversity of this secluded woodland. Resident mammals include white-tailed deer, gray fox, raccoons and bobcats. Ruffed grouse and wild turkey may be spotted along the trail.

The area is accessed by a 13 mile backpack trail, the **Wildcat Trail**, which, considering the topography, is a bit long for a day hike. Fortunately, a **Connecting Trail** bisects the loop and yields a more reasonable distance of 5 miles.

Trail Route:

From the parking lot, the **Wildcat Trail** leads northward, crosses Eel's Run and winds through a fragrant stand of pine. At the next stream crossing the trail forks; the trail to the right is the return route from the Cedar Run/Wildcat Hollow side of the backpack loop. Bypass this trail and proceed northward, crossing the side stream and then re-crossing Eel's Run. The route continues toward the northwest, climbing steadily as it leads upstream. It eventually cuts away from the creek and ascends from the ravine, emerging onto Irish Ridge Road.

Hike northward along the road for a short distance and watch for an old jeep trail on your right. This is the **Connecting Trail**. Hike eastward along this wide path and, within ½ mile, you will intersect the east arm of the **Wildcat Trail** backpack loop.

Turn right, hiking along the crest of the ridge. Wildcat Hollow will be on your left while the Eel's Run basin drops away to your right. The trail winds toward the southeast and then angles directly to the south. After hiking atop the ridge for 1.5 miles, you will begin a gentle descent into a side ravine of the Eel's Run Valley. Another .5 mile brings you back to the intersection with the entry trail. Turn left for a short walk to the parking area.

Directions:

From Corning, Ohio, on S.R. 13, proceed eastward and uphill on the road that is the east extension of S.R. 155. At the top of the hill, bear right and drive approximately 2 miles along County Road 70 (also called Waterworks Road). This road deadends into County Road 16 (Irish Ridge Road). Turn right (south), drive 1.4 miles and turn left on another County Road. Proceed 1.5 miles to the Wildcat Hollow parking area, on your left.

Winter on the Wildcat Trail

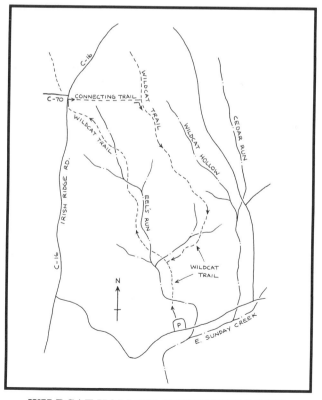

WILDCAT HOLLOW (SOUTHERN LOOP)

54 HOCKING STATE PARK
Ash Cave - Cedar Falls - Old Man's Cave

Distance: Day hikes of 5.0, 7.0 and 12.0 miles
Terrain: hilly; moderate grades; stairways

There is broad consensus that the Hocking Region of south-central Ohio harbors the most spectacular scenery in the State. Untouched by glaciers, the area's numerous streams have carved a myriad of caves, gorges, rock cliffs and natural bridges from the Blackhand sandstone that underlies the region's thin soil. Deposited in shallow seas during the Mississippian Period, this resistant bedrock, overlying softer layers of limestone and shale, predisposes to the formation of waterfalls and recessed caves.

The cool, shaded gorges protect vast stands of hemlock and a variety of ferns thrive in these moist ravines. Dry, rocky slopes are cloaked by a mixed forest of oak, hickory and pine, typical of the Appalachian Plateau.

Two thousand acres of Hocking State Forest have been set aside as a State Park; the Park is comprised of four tracts, stretching north to south through the Forest. Access is provided by an extensive network of trails. A six-mile section of the **Buckeye Trail (BT)**, known locally as the **Granny Gatewood Trail**, connects the Old Man's Cave, Cedar Falls and Ash Cave areas. A long, 12 mile day hike can thus be accomplished by completing the roundtrip course from either end but most visitors would likely prefer the shorter options described below. The Old Man's Cave area is usually the most congested site (especially on autumn weekends) and I recommend parking at either Cedar Falls or Ash Cave.

Cantwell Cliffs, the northernmost section of Hocking State Park, is covered in Hike #56.

Trail Routes:

Ash Cave to Cedar Falls (5 miles roundtrip). From the Ash Cave parking lot, hike northward on the trail that leads upstream across the floor of the gorge. This .3 mile section is now being paved to provide access for handicapped visitors. The trail winds along the stream, crossing it at several points, and soon leads to the base of Ash Cave and its 90-foot cascade. Before you are the largest recessed cave and the highest waterfall in Ohio.

After a respite at this scenic haven, hike behind the falls and climb onto the eastern wall of the gorge via a stairway. Turn left, cross the stream and follow the blue-blazed **Buckeye Trail** as it leads northward, gradually ascending along the creek bed. After hiking about 1 mile you will cross a power line swath and soon thereafter reach County Road 255.

Cross the road and follow the trail as it veers to the left and descends into the next ravine. Another .5 mile walk takes you across the stream and into a clearing where an abandoned roadbed crosses from west to east. Turn right and follow this jeep trail, ascending to the Cedar Falls area. Hike across the parking loop and descend into the Cedar Falls basin along a side ravine. The trail leads across a bridge in front of the Falls, offering a splendid view of the cascade.

Return to Ash Cave via the same route, completing a roundtrip hike of 5 miles.

Ash Cave

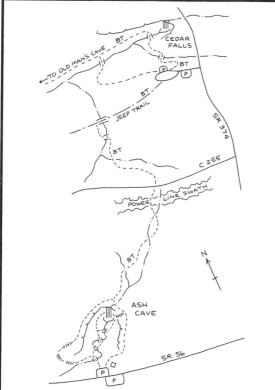

**ASH CAVE
TO
CEDAR FALLS**

Cedar Falls to Old Man's Cave Area (7 miles roundtrip). Park at the Cedar Falls access area and descend to the Falls along a side ravine (see map). Cross the bridge and follow the **Buckeye Trail** as it leads westward, paralleling the bank of Queer Creek. A 1.5 mile hike brings you to an intersection where the **Gulf Trail (GT)** leads off to the left. Bear right and proceed northward toward the Old Man's Cave Area. As the gorge begins to narrow you will come to the Lower Falls, a beautiful waterfall, framed by sandstone cliffs and hemlock forest.

Climb around the east side of the cascade and begin a one mile hike to the Upper Falls through the narrow, rock-walled gorge. Old Man's Cave, a huge recess in the cliff wall, will be noted on your left (see map). Stay along the floor of the gorge until you reach the Upper Falls at the north end of the chasm.

For your return trip, ascend to the east rim and hike southward to the A-frame Bridge (A). Cross to the west rim and turn left. Walk a short distance and descend through Old Man's Cave, named for Richard Rowe who lived in this natural shelter during the late 1800s. The "Sphinx Head (S)" rises just south of the Cave, towering above the Lower Falls. Descend to the floor of the gorge and retrace your route to Cedar Falls, completing a roundtrip hike of 7 miles.

Directions:

The Ash Cave parking lots are located along S.R. 56, 12.5 miles east of Laurelville (4 miles east of S. Bloomingville). The Cedar Falls lot is west of S.R. 374, 2 miles north of S.R. 56 (or 2 miles south of S.R. 664). The Old Man's Cave parking area is on S.R. 664, approximately 4.5 miles northeast of S. Bloomingville (or 10.5 miles west of U.S. 33).

View from Old Man's Cave

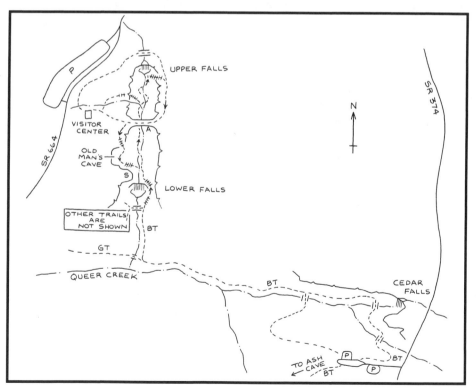

CEDAR FALLS TO OLD MAN'S CAVE

55 CONKLES HOLLOW STATE NATURE PRESERVE

Distance: Day hikes of 1.0, 2.0 and 3.0 miles
Terrain: flat within gorge; steep ascent and descent to rim

Conkles Hollow, in the Hocking Hills region of south-central Ohio, harbors, in my opinion, the most spectacular landscape in our State. A hike through its scenic gorge, especially on a crisp October day, is a feast for the senses. Autumn colors contrast with the deep green of the hemlocks, all set against the backdrop of white, sandstone cliffs and a brilliant blue sky. Moisture-laden air, perfumed by the abundant moss, highlights the sun beams as they pierce the depths of the gorge. Waterfalls spring from the rocky walls and numerous ferns cling to the sandstone ledges.

Dedicated as a State Nature Preserve in April, 1977, Conkles Hollow is named for W. J. Conkle, who chiseled his/her name on the wall of the gorge in 1797. The inscription has since worn away but the natural beauty of this secluded refuge has changed little in the past 200 years.

Trail Routes:

Access to the Preserve is provided by two superb trails. The **Gorge Trail (A)** winds through the floor of the chasm, crossing and recrossing the stream that carved this spectacular gorge. Sheer cliffs of Blackhand sandstone, dating from the Mississippian Period, rise 200 feet above the creek. Huge slumps blocks, having broken away from the rugged canyon walls, rest along the valley floor. The cool, moist ravines harbor ferns, yew and teaberry while the sunny, dry slopes are cloaked by an oak-pine forest.

The **Gorge Trail** is .5 mile in length and leads from the parking area to the north end of the canyon, where the stream plunges down from higher terrain. Half way along its course, a spur trails up to Diagonal Cave (see map), a huge recess in the gorge wall. A roundtrip hike along the **Gorge Trail** yields a distance of 1.0 mile.

The **Rim Trail (B)** is a 2.0 mile, elongated loop atop the gorge walls. Winding near the edge of the cliffs, this route offers a different perspective of the chasm, yielding spectacular views into its depths. The **Rim Trail** is accessed via stairways and switchbacks at the south end of the gorge (see map).

Combining the **Rim Trail** loop with a roundtrip hike on the **Gorge Trail** yields a total distance of 3.0 miles.

Directions:

From Laurelville, drive east on S.R. 180 for 7 miles. Turn right (south) on S.R. 374 and drive another 6 miles. Turn left (east) on Big Pine Road and proceed .2 mile to the parking area, on your left. If possible, plan a weekday visit; weekend crowds, especially large in October, can detract from the serenity of this natural gem.

146

Sunbeams pierce the cool depths of the gorge.

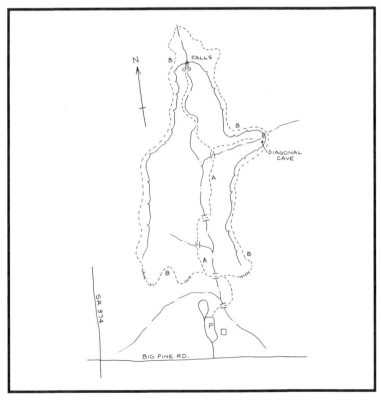

CONKLES HOLLOW NATURE PRESERVE

56 CANTWELL CLIFFS

Distance: 1.5 miles
Terrain: hilly; steep climbs

Our concept of time is rooted in the human lifespan, a mere instant in the course of earth's history. It is thus difficult to comprehend the geologic events that have culminated in the varied landforms that we find across the globe today. The scenic wonders of the Hocking region are certainly no exception.

Deposited in shallow seas during the Mississippian Period, the famous Blackhand sandstone of south-central Ohio was uplifted with the Appalachian Plateau as Africa and North America collided, some 250 million years ago. Since that time, water erosion has gradually carved the gorges, recessed caves, natural bridges and rock formations that now characterize the area. Protected from the Pleistocene ice sheets, the Hocking region harbors some of the most scenic topography in our State,

Cantwell Cliffs, the northernmost province of Hocking State Park, protects a rugged gorge, carved into the Mississippian bedrock by a network of streams. Trails lead into the gorge and along its rim, offering spectacular views of the Preserve's waterfalls and of sandstone cliffs that tower almost 100 feet above the valley floor. The route described below yields a total hike of 1.5 miles.

Trail Route:

Follow the westernmost entry trail that leads north from the parking lot and passes to the left (west) of the shelter house (1). You will soon descend a long set of rock stairs and arrive at the intersection with the **Rim Trail (RT)**. Cross this trail and descend into the gorge via a narrow, steep stairway that drops through a fracture in the rock wall. Leveling out along a terrace, the trail passes another narrow fracture on your right, known as the "Fat Woman's Squeeze (2)." Cut through this passage (if you can), descend a short path and turn back to your left, winding up the base of Cantwell's highest waterfall (3).

Circle behind the falls, passing beneath a huge, recessed cave, and begin a gradual descent downstream along the **Gorge Trail (GT)**. Hike along the north bank for about ¼ mile and then cross the stream via a small bridge. Turn left, walk about 50 yards and bear left at the trail intersection, continuing downstream. The trail soon forks, creating a .5 mile loop through the lower, more open section of the gorge. Bear left at the fork, cross the creek and wind downstream along its north bank. This branch of the loop stays near the level of the stream and crosses a tributary along the way.

At the end of the loop the trail curves southward, crossing the primary stream and a side channel. Bridges are not present at this crossing and high water can present a challenge. Once across, follow the trail as it parallels the sidestream and then curves westward, climbing onto the wall of the gorge. Twenty to thirty feet above the valley floor, the trail undulates westward, crossing through a dense stand of hemlock. Descending gradually, you will soon return to the origin of the loop. Continue westward and turn left at the next trail intersection, climbing through a side ravine of the gorge.

Near the waterfall (4) the trail forks; bear right and cross the stream in front of the falls. The trail leads upward onto the west wall of the ravine and then curves to the north, hugging the rocky outcrops that line the rim of the gorge. At the next intersection turn left and climb a sandstone stairway to the **Rim Trail**. Turn right along this flat path and you will soon be treated to a breathtaking view of a third waterfall (5), hemmed in by sheer cliffs of rock. A return trail to the parking lot angles southward from this site (see map).

*A view from
the rim*

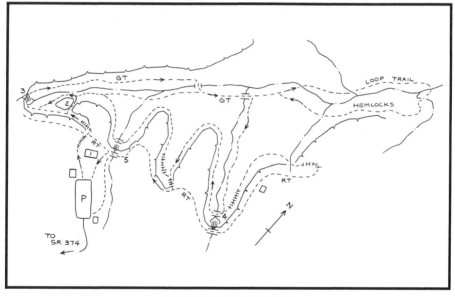

CANTWELL CLIFFS

Directions:

Cantwell Cliffs is east of S.R. 374 and north of S.R. 180. From Laurelville, follow S.R. 180 east for 11.7 miles and turn left (north) on S.R. 374. Drive 1.5 miles to the Park, on your right.

From U.S. 33, drive west on S.R. 180 for 4.2 miles and turn right (north) onto S.R. 374. Proceed 1.5 miles to the Park.

57 GREAT SEAL STATE PARK

Distance: Day hikes of 2.1, 2.5 and 8.6 miles
Terrain: hilly; steep climbs and descents

Established in 1980, Great Seal is one of Ohio's younger State Parks. Characterized by a chain of wooded knobs and ridges, just north of Chillicothe, the Park is named for the fact that these same hills inspired the design of Ohio's emblem (the Great Seal of Ohio).

Situated near the western edge of the Appalachian Plateau, these highlands offer expansive views across the Scioto Valley to the west and south. However, heavy forest cover restricts the view in most areas and vistas are broader during the winter months.

Great Seal's 20-mile network of hiking and horseback trails wind up and down across the component ridges. There is only modest use of switchbacks and some climbs are very steep. Hiking at this Park should be reserved for fit and experienced persons. Ridgetops are generally 400-500 feet higher than the parking areas.

Trail Routes:

The map depicts the layout of Great Seal's trail network. Green intersection markers (letters on the map) are placed throughout the Park.

The **Sugarloaf Mountain Trail (B-A-B)** is a 2.1 mile loop that includes a steep ascent of Sugarloaf Mountain, the most northern knob in the Park.

The **Shawnee Ridge Trail (B-C-D-E-K-L-C)** is 7.8 miles in length and involves the ascent and descent of Bald Hill and Sand Hill. Completing the round trip back to the parking lot at the base of Sugarloaf Moun-

tain yields a total distance of 8.6 miles.

For the best views in the Park I recommend a 2.5 mile section of the **Mt. Eyes Trail**. The latter, **E-F-G-H-I-J**, has a total length of 6.4 miles. Start at the small parking area off Lick Run Road, .9 mile south of Rocky Road (see map). Enter the trail at Point I and hike northward along the stream for a short distance. Crossing the creek, the trail begins a steep climb onto the saddle between Bunker Hill and Mt. Eyes. At Point H, a faint trail leads north onto the Bunker Hill ridge. Bear left and cross the saddle before enduring another steep climb onto Mt. Eyes. The lowlands of the Chillicothe basin begin to unfold to the south and a few clearings offer splendid views of the other Great Seal ridges to the north. Hike eastward along the crest of Mt. Eyes and then descend toward the north via a winding route.

A large clearcut area opens the view to the southeast and provides an excellent site for observing native wildlife. At the bottom of the slope the trail veers to the right, crosses the stream and exits onto Lick Run Road at Point G. Turn left for a short hike back to your car.

Directions:

Follow S.R. 159 north from Chillicothe. Cross over U.S. 23 and proceed another 1.3 miles. Turn right (east) onto Delano Road. Drive 1 mile and turn right onto Marietta Road, which runs along the west edge of the Park. Proceed to parking areas as illustrated on the map.

Looking north from Mt. Eyes

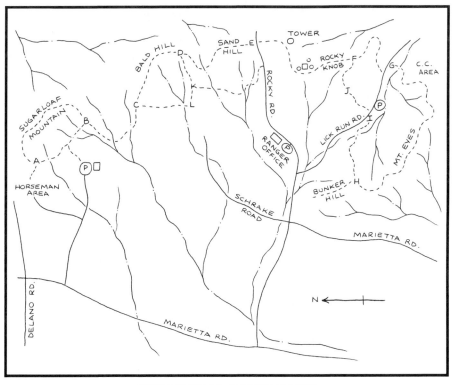

GREAT SEAL STATE PARK

58 TAR HOLLOW STATE PARK & FOREST

Distance: Day hikes of 3.0 and 11.5 miles
Terrain: hilly; steep areas on Logan Trail

Looking out from Tar Hollow's Brush Ridge Fire Tower, the numerous ridgetops of southeastern Ohio are remarkably uniform in elevation. This feature typifies the Appalachian Plateau, which stretches from the Catskills of New York through western Pennsylvania, eastern Ohio, most of West Virginia, eastern Kentucky and central Tennessee. Similar topography is seen in the Ozarks of Missouri/Arkansas and across the Colorado Plateau of the American Southwest.

In each of these regions, the ridges (mesas in the Southwest) have been carved from an uplifted plateau by water erosion. Numerous streams, dendritic in pattern, course through the tabletop landscape, yielding a vast network of valleys and ravines. In the eastern U.S., where rainfall is abundant, the ridges are "rounded off" and covered by forest. By contrast, arid conditions across the Colorado Plateau have resulted in a stark, rugged land of deep canyons and rock "monuments."

Tar Hollow State Forest cloaks over 16,000 acres of the Appalachian Plateau and is home to Tar Hollow State Park. The area is accessed via an extensive network of hiking trails and bridal paths. A section of the **Buckeye Trail (BT)** cuts through the center of the Forest. Day hikers should consider the following two routes:

Trail Routes:

Brush Ridge Trail (BRT). This 1.5 mile trail (3.0 miles roundtrip) starts at the Pine Lake picnic area, along Tar Hollow Road (Forest Road #10) and ascends to the Brush Ridge Fire Tower (FT). The initial section is moderately steep but switchbacks ease your climb onto the ridge. The trail loops around the upper end of several ravines before winding across the crest of the ridge to the Fire Tower. The latter offers a panorama of the Tar Hollow region. Descend to Pine Lake via the same route for a total hike of 3.0 miles.

North Loop of Logan Trail (NLT). Adventurous and conditioned hikers may want to complete the entire 11.5 mile circuit of the **North Loop of the Logan Trail.** Beginning at the Pine Lake picnic area, the first 1.5 mile section of this loop is covered by the **Brush Ridge Trail (BRT)**, described above. From the Fire Tower, the **Logan Trail**, blazed with red slashes, angles toward the northwest and soon forks into the South and North Loops. Bear right onto the **North Loop** and begin a strenuous hike back to Pine Lake.

The trail makes a long descent into Slickaway Hollow, followed by a steep ascent onto the next ridge. Staying near the crest of the ridge, the trail winds to the east of the next ravine, continues northward and then turns sharply to the right, descending into a ravine and crossing Forest Road #16.

Climbing onto the edge of the next ridge, the trail parallels Road #16, heading northwest, and then turns to the northeast, ascending through a long ravine. Near the ridgetop, the trail cuts back to the south, crosses the North Ridge Road (Road #4) and begins a 2-mile descent through Tar Hollow. Nearing the campgrounds, bear left at several intersections, where spur trails yield access to campers. The **North Loop** eventually climbs onto another ridge, traverses the crest and makes a steep descent to Road #10 and the Pine Lake picnic area.

Directions:

The Pine Lake Picnic Area is reached via Tar Hollow Road (Forest Road #10) which leads westward from S.R. 327. To reach this intersection, follow S.R. 327 south for 7 miles from Adelphi, or north for 9.6 miles from Londonderry.

The Brush Ridge Fire Tower

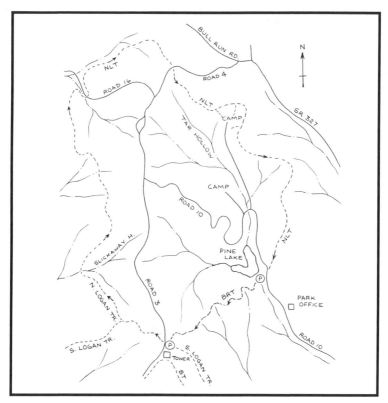

NORTH LOOP OF LOGAN TRAIL

59 LAKE HOPE STATE PARK

Distance: Day hikes of 6.0 and 7.4 miles
Terrain: rolling

Lake Hope State Park, established in 1949, occupies the former site of a thriving iron production center. Hope Furnace Station was one of 80 iron communities that sprung up across the "Hanging Rock Iron Belt" of southern Ohio and northeastern Kentucky during the mid 1800s. Today, only the remnant furnace structures attest to that vibrant but short-lived economy.

Iron ore, extracted from the Pennsylvanian sandstone that underlies the region, was combined with charcoal and limestone in the huge furnaces. This smelting process trapped impurities in the limestone "flux" and the heavier, molten iron was drained into sand molds to cool. Production of the charcoal for the furnaces resulted in the destruction of many acres of timber across the Iron Belt.

Other artifacts from the Hope Furnace glory days now lie entombed beneath the waters of Lake Hope, impounded by the damming of Raccoon Creek in 1938. Fortunately, the denuded forests have recovered and abundant wildlife, including the industrious beaver, has returned to the area. A visit to the State Park and surrounding State Forest (see Hike #60) offers a retreat to the natural beauty of Ohio's pre-industrial era.

Trail Route:

Fifteen miles of hiking trails provide access to the Park's remote areas. The following route utilizes the **Hope Furnace Trail**, perhaps the most popular and scenic hike at the Park, which covers a distance of 3 miles along the north and west shores of Lake Hope.

Park at the Hope Furnace lot on the north side of S.R. 278. Hike northwestward through the open picnic area and pick up the **Hope Furnace Trail (A)** as it winds along a scenic backwater marsh. Ascending to somewhat higher ground, the trail begins its 3-mile excursion along the lakeshore. Much of the route is level but stream crossings can be tricky after wet weather. Views of Lake Hope are constant along the way and eastern hemlocks grace the shaded coves. Watch for signs of beaver activity near the inlet streams.

The **Hope Furnace Trail** ends at Picnic Point, near the southwestern end of the lake. You may wish to stop here for rest and nourishment, returning via the same route for a roundtrip hike of 6.0 miles.

An alternative return route is to hike around the Dam area via Park Roads 12 and 9 (see map) and then walk northeastward along S.R. 278 to the entrance for the Lodge and Cabins (Road #1). Just in from Route 278, turn left onto the **Peninsula Trail (B)** which follows the eastern shore of Lake Hope and circles back to the road near the Hope Furnace. This complete loop around Lake Hope yields a total hike of 7.4 miles.

Directions:

Lake Hope State Park straddles S.R. 278, approximately 8 miles north of Prattsville (on U.S. 50) or 5 miles south of S.R. 56 (14 miles west of Athens). Refer to the map for the location of parking areas.

Autumn along the Lake

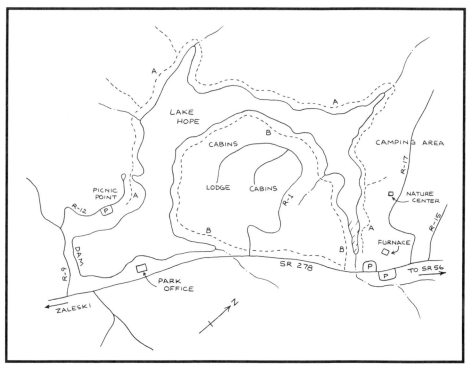

LAKE HOPE STATE PARK

60 ZALESKI STATE FOREST

Distance: Day hikes of 6.6 and 10.0 miles
Terrain: hilly; steep areas

Zaleski State Forest, encompassing much of eastern Vinton County, is an attractive refuge for wildlife and hikers alike. A 23.5 mile **Backpack Trail** winds through the Forest and its ten-mile southern loop is recommended for day hikes. Blazed with orange-red slashes, this trail is accessed from parking areas along S.R. 278, near the Hope Furnace, at Lake Hope State Park.

Trail Route:

From the parking lots, walk west along S.R. 278 for a short distance and watch for the common trailhead for the **Backpack Trail (BPT)** and **Olds Hollow Trail (OHT)** on the south side of the road. The trails cross a drainage channel and then turn eastward, rising through a cool, pine forest. Beavers have created a series of ponds and marshes along the streambed north of the trail and gnawed tree stumps are evident throughout the area.

The trail dips through a side ravine, continues eastward and enters a deeper ravine where the **Olds Hollow Trail** splits to the south. The **Backpack Trail** climbs eastward and then descends toward King Hollow Road, where the **Connecting Trail (CT)**, blazed with white, comes in from the north. The **Backpack Trail** swings to the southeast and begins a direct assault on the ridge, climbing 200 feet in less than ¼ mile. Once atop the hill, the trail levels out and begins a 2.5 mile excursion along high ground, staying on or near the crest of the ridge. White-tailed deer are common along the sunny slopes and ruffed grouse often flush as you hike along the trail. Pileated woodpeckers seem especially common in this remote forest.

After hiking about 1 mile along the ridge, you will pass a backpackers campground (designated Area C). The trail angles to the right, following a southward extension of the ridge. Another 1.5 mile brings you to a spectacular overlook, 300 feet above the Hewett Fork of Raccoon Creek. Gnarled pines cling to the thin soil and the open canopy offers a broad view across the gorge. Watch for skinks that often sun themselves on the cliffside rocks. Many hikers choose this point as their destination and, after a picnic lunch at the overlook, return to the parking lot via the same route. This yields a total roundtrip distance of 6.6 miles.

Should you decide to continue the 10 mile loop, the **Backpack Trail** angles northward and descends into a deep ravine. It then follows the stream to the valley floor where it crosses the site of an abandoned mining town, Ingham Station (site #3). Turning north again, the trail climbs onto the next ridge. Another .5 mile takes you past a prehistoric ceremonial mound (Point #5), constructed by the Adena culture, approximately 2000 years ago.

Past the mound, the trail turns eastward and, after looping past Campground D, descends into King Hollow. Climbing onto the next hill, you begin a two mile hike toward the northwest, staying near the crest of the ridge. As the trail descends along the wall of a ravine, watch for the white-blazed **Connecting Trail** on your left (at Point F). This winds to the southwest, crosses King Hollow and merges with the south arm of the **Backpack Trail** loop. Turn right and return to the parking area, retracing your entry route.

Directions:

The parking areas for the south loop of the Backpack Trail are located on either side of S.R. 278, 8.3 miles north of Prattsville (arriving via U.S. 50) or 4.7 miles south of the S.R. 56 junction (14 miles west of Athens).

Wind-battered pines at the Hewett Fork overlook

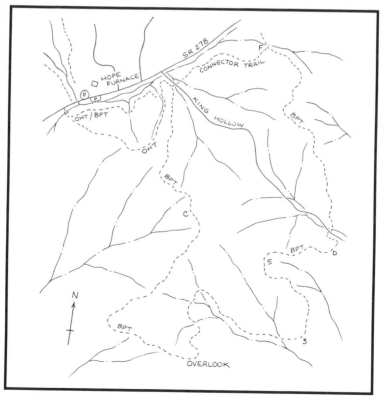

THE SOUTH LOOP OF THE BACKPACK TRAIL

61 STROUDS RUN STATE PARK

Distance: Day hikes of 2.0, 7.0 and 10.0 miles
Terrain: flat/rolling lakeshore; hilly side loops

If it's serenity that you seek, consider an off-season visit to Strouds Run State Park. Five miles east of Athens, the Park's 2606 acres are centered around a 161 acre lake. Fishing, swimming and picnic activity peak during the warmer months and, due to the Park's isolation from major roads, Strouds Run is sparsely utilized from November through March.

Access to the Park's trail system is provided by parking lots along County Road #20 and at the Beach Area (see map). The Park Office is located on Township Road #212, one mile north of the lake.

Trail Routes:
The 7-mile **Lakeview Trail (A)** winds along the shoreline of Dow Lake. Except for a few stream crossings and short hill climbs (especially near the dam), the route is generally flat. Lake views are constant along the way and the route crosses varied habitat of forest, meadow and marsh.

The **Indian Mound (C), Sycamore Valley (D)** and **Pioneer Cemetery (E)** side trails are each approximately 1 mile in length. The addition of these routes to the **Lakeview Trail** thus bring your hike to a distance of 10 miles.

The green-blazed **Broken Rock Trail (B)**, 2 miles in length, provides a demanding side excursion for the conditioned hiker. The trail's steep ascent and descent across the valley wall are accomplished with little attention to the concept of switchbacks. Nevertheless, rocky outcroppings, deep ravines and one scenic overlook (see map) reward your effort. The **Lookout Trail (LT)** bissects the **Broken Rock** loop, offering an even steeper route.

Before leaving the Park, you may want to explore the banks of Strouds Run, north of the lake. Beavers have colonized the area and their dams and lodges can be found along the stream. The engineers themselves are best observed at dusk.

Directions:
Take the Chauncey/Amesville Exit from U.S. 33 on the east side of Athens. Follow Columbus Road southwest (toward Athens), drive 2 miles and turn left onto Lancaster Road. Proceed one block and bear right onto Columbia. Follow this road for 3.5 miles to Strouds Run Park. The route cuts through a residential area, crosses over U.S. 33, angles to the right and then curves eastward to the Park.

View from Broken Rock Trail

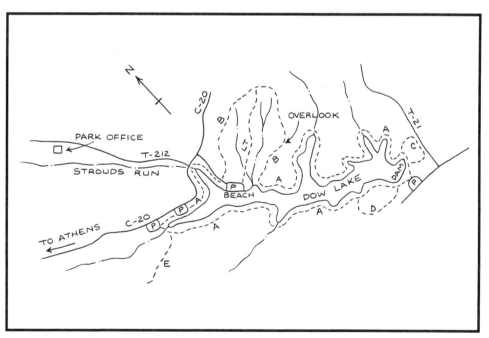

STROUDS RUN STATE PARK

62 SCIOTO TRAIL STATE PARK

Distance: Day hikes of 3.5 and 4.6 miles
Terrain: hilly; some steep areas

Five miles north of Waverly, Ohio, a ridge of high ground stretches eastward toward the Scioto River Valley. The eastern end of this ridge, dissected by Stoney Creek and its tributaries, provides a beautiful setting for Scioto Trail State Park and State Forest.

This area, named for the River's 2000 year contribution to human navigation, offers excellent hiking opportunities. A portion of the Buckeye Trail cuts through southern sections of the Forest and is accessed by a spur trail from the Stewart Lake camping area (see map).

Day hikes are best pursued from the parking area just north of Caldwell Lake. Due to the ridge/valley topography, all routes are hilly and some steep areas will be encountered. However, the trails are wide, well-marked and well-maintained. The following two day hikes are recommended.

Trail Routes:

A. **Caldwell Lake/Fire Tower Loop.** This 4.6 mile, moderately strenuous hike starts just west of the parking lot at the north end of Caldwell Lake. Follow the trail as it leads into the forest and ascends the ridge between Stoney Creek and its North Fork. The 1.75 mile ascent to Forest Road #3 follows the crest of the ridge and views are extensive during the colder months. After hiking .75 mile a side trail descends southward to the Stewart Lake area; should you decide to shorten your loop by taking this trail, be advised that the middle section is very steep.

To proceed to the Fire Tower (F), bypass this cutoff and continue westward along the ridge. Another ½ mile of hiking brings you to a side loop to the Debord Vista. This ridgetop clearing yields a broad view when weather and foliage conditions are favorable. Return to the main trail and continue westward for another ½ mile to Forest Road #3.

Turn left (south) along the roadway for a gradual, .5 mile ascent to the Forest Headquarters (HQ) and Fire Tower (F). The latter can be climbed and provides a sweeping view of the Appalachian Plateau and its countless ridges.

The descent back to Caldwell Lake begins behind a maintenance building, just north of the Forest Headquarters (see map). The trail parallels Forest Road #1, rolling along the edge of the woods. The descent is steep in some areas, especially along the Sled Hill near Stewart Lake. Once past this slope, the terrain begins to flatten out though an undulating course continues all the way to North Fork creek. Approximately 1.5 miles east of the Fire Tower the trail crosses a small parking lot that services the Park's 1-mile Nature Trail (NT). Continue eastward for another .4 mile and turn northward along the North Fork of Stoney Creek. Hike along the west shore of Caldwell Lake and return to the parking lot.

B. **Combination of Church Hollow and Triple-C Loops.** These two trail loops wind across the eastern wall of the North Fork Valley. From the parking area north of Caldwell Lake, cross Forest Road #3 and follow the narrow lane that enters the campground (see map). Walk approximately 25 yards and find the trailhead for the **Church Hollow Trail**, to your left. This loop follows the Creek upstream for about one mile and then turns eastward, circling back across the hillside.

Once back at the campground, switch to the **CCC Trail** for a second loop through the forest. The last section of this trail parallels a side stream and descends to the eastern shore of Caldwell Lake. Turn right along Forest Road #3 and return to the parking lot or cross the dam and return along the west shore of the Lake. This combined hike yields a total distance of 3.5 miles.

Morning mist shrouds the ridgetops of Scioto Trail State Forest.

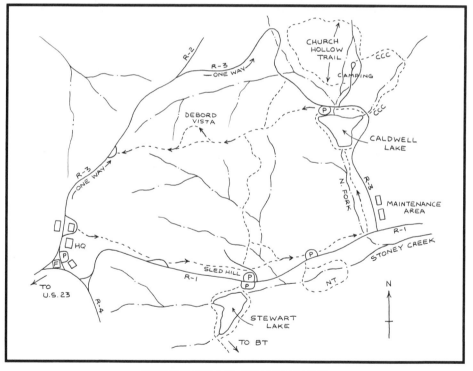

SCIOTO TRAIL STATE PARK

Directions:

Scioto Trail State Park lies east of U.S. 23, 5.5 miles north of Waverly (11.5 miles south of Chillicothe). Follow S.R. 372 east from U.S. 23 and proceed .5 mile to the Park. Refer to map for the location of parking areas.

63 LAKE KATHARINE STATE NATURE PRESERVE

Distance: 4.5 miles
Terrain: hilly; stairways, steep areas

Providing shelter from the heat of summer and the frigid winds of winter, the Rock Run Gorge of Lake Katharine State Nature Preserve harbors both northern and southern plant species. Within it narrow chasm are dense stands of hemlock, pockets of mountain laurel and the northernmost population of bigleaf magnolia. Rare and endangered wildflowers, including starflower, mountain watercress and stemless lady's slipper, carpet the gorge during late April and May.

Located a few miles northwest of Jackson, the Preserve's western sections are closed to the public. However, three excellent trails provide access to the Rock Run Gorge, its adjacent ridges and sections of the Little Salt Creek floodplain. The following route yields a 4.5 mile hike through this scenic refuge.

Trail Route:

From the parking lot, walk to the northwest and pick up the **Pine Ridge (A)** and **Calico Bush (B) Trails**. Wind to the west, crossing behind the Ranger's residence (1) and descend through sandstone ledges that jut from the upper gorge wall. Below the rock outcroppings the trail forks; the **Calico Bush Trail (B)** curves to the right and begins a one mile loop along the south wall of the gorge, eventually climbing back to the parking area (see map).

Bear left and continue along the **Pine Ridge Trail (A)** as it winds deeper into the gorge and arrives at the east end of Lake Katharine. After enjoying the view of this scenic lake, cross the dam and adjacent spillway (2). The latter uses a fracture in the sandstone wall, where water tumbles over the polished rock and funnels into the narrow gorge.

Climb the northern wall of Rock Run Gorge, crossing through an area of huge hemlock trees. Many seem to grow right from the honeycombed sandstone. Cross a tributary of Rock Run Creek and ascend higher onto the ridge where the forest is dominated by tall pines. For the next mile the **Pine Ridge Trail** leads eastward above the gorge, winding past a scenic waterfall (3) and looping out to a clifftop overlook (4).

Nearing the east end of the ridge, the trail snakes down to the floodplain of Little Salt Creek and heads upstream. Wood ducks are often found in this area. After crossing Rock Run, the trail ascends onto the south wall of the gorge where it joins the **Calico Bush Trail (B)**. Continue toward the south and, at the next intersection, bear left onto the **Salt Creek Trail (C)**.

Constructed by the Youth Conservation Corps during the late 1970s, the 2 mile **Salt Creek** loop is renowned for its use of catwalks, stairways and natural terraces. After winding toward the creek, the trail cuts back to the west, crossing through a fissure in the rock wall. It then hugs the cliff, traversing wooden stairways and passing beneath sandstone ledges.

At the next intersection a **Shortcut (D)** ascends from the gorge and leads back toward the parking area. Bear left and continue along the **Salt Creek Trail (C)** as it zig-zags across the floodplain of Little Salt Creek, using a series of boardwalks (5). After looping westward to cross a sidestream, the trail returns to the bank of the Creek. Here another grove of hemlocks, set against sandstone cliffs, adds to the scenic beauty.

Turning away from the creek, the trail curves to the northwest and begins a long, steady climb out of the gorge. After recrossing the sidestream the route makes one more loop through the hemlocks, cuts through the ridgetop pine forest and merges with the **Shortcut Trail (D)**. A short hike from here takes you out of the woods and along a meadow to the parking area.

A view through the spillway.

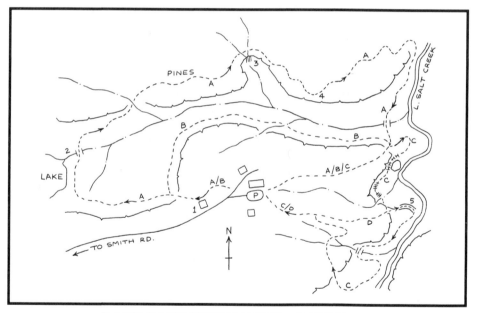

LAKE KATHARINE NATURE PRESERVE

Directions:

From Jackson, on S.R. 93, turn west onto Bridge St. (this is about 2 blocks north of the County Building). Proceed 1 block and bear right onto State St., which becomes County Road 76. Drive 1.8 miles and turn right (north) on Smith Road (County Road 60). Proceed 1.5 miles and bear right onto the entry road of Lake Katharine State Nature Preserve.

163

64 LAKE VESUVIUS RECREATION AREA

Distance: Day hikes of 7.5, 8.0, 11.0 and 12.0 miles
Terrain: rolling along lakeshore; hilly with some steep
areas along Backpack Trail

The Lake Vesuvius Recreation Area, located in the southernmost section of Wayne National Forest, owes its existence to the reclamation of an abandoned iron production center. One of eighty such communities across the Hanging Rock Iron Belt of southeastern Ohio/northeastern Kentucky, Vesuvius produced iron from 1833 to 1906. During that period, much of the local forest was destroyed as timber was converted to charcoal for use in the smelting furnaces. The idle Vesuvious Furnace (F) still stands near the spillway of the Lake.

By the 1930s, plans were underway to restore the area and, in 1939, the Dam across Storm's Creek was completed. Second and third growth forest now cloaks the ridges though timber harvesting still continues in the region. The Recreation Area provides facilities for campers, fishermen, boaters, horseback riders, hikers and picnicers. A small museum (M) is open during the warmer months and serves as an education center.

Trail Routes:

Lake Vesuvius Recreation Area offers an excellent network of trails. A 16 mile **Backpack Trail (BPT)**, blazed with yellow diamonds, winds across the ridgetops that surround the Lake basin. The 8 mile **Lakeshore Trail (LST)**, blazed with white diamonds, snakes along the shoreline, crossing inlet streams and passing scenic rock formations that rise above the lake. Both of these trails are accessed via the Boat Dock Parking Area, just northwest of the Dam (see map). Other parking areas, in more remote sections of the preserve, are not frequently patrolled and are thus not recommended. The followng day hikes are suggested:

Lakeshore Trail. The most scenic and popular hike at Vesuvius, this 8 mile trail hugs the shoreline for most of its route. Blazed with white diamonds, the trail begins at the Boat Dock parking area. Since it is a loop trail, one may choose to hike in either direction. Lakeside pine woodlands and outcroppings of sandstone make southern sections of the loop especially scenic.

Western loop of Backpack Trail. By using the **Aldrich Cutoff Trail (ACT)**, one may reduce the **Backpack Trail (BPT)** to a 12 mile loop . . . still a long day hike. Follow the west arm of the **Lakeshore Trail (LST)** for almost one mile and watch for the **Backpack Trail** as it forks to the left and ascends along the wall of the basin. A gradual one-mile climb takes you across the Beach access road and you then begin a 4-mile stroll along the crest of the ridge that divides the Vesuvius (Storm's Creek) basin from the valley of Big Cannons Creek, to the north. Passing mile marker #5, you will curve to the southeast and descend into Aldrich Hollow.

Watch for the **Aldrich Cutoff Trail (ACT)** on your right and follow it downstream toward Storm's Creek. Within ½ mile you will intersect the east arm of the **Backpack Trail.** Turn right, hike almost one mile along the creek and then veer left, joining the **Lakeshore Trail** and crossing the stream.

After another .5 mile the **Lakeshore Trail** splits to the right. Continue southward on the **Backpack Trail**, climbing through a ravine. Crossing the side stream, ascend to the crest of the hill and begin a 2-mile hike atop the ridge. You will pass through a clearcut area, cross over the Iron Ridge Campground Road and eventually return to the Dam area. Descend several stairways, rejoin the **Lakeshore Trail,** cross the Dam and return to the Boat Ramp parking area.

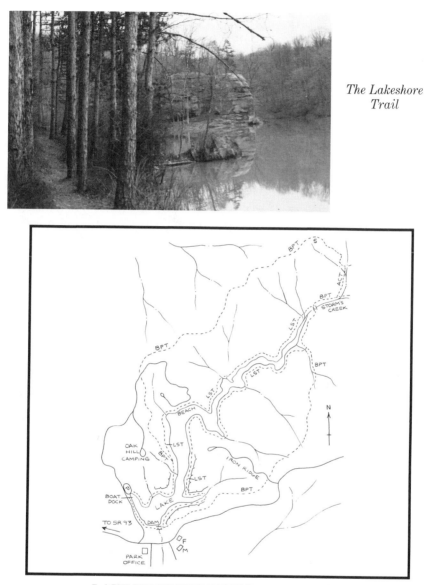

The Lakeshore Trail

LAKE VESUVIUS RECREATION AREA

Combination Routes: Since the **Lakeshore Tail** and the **Backpack Trail** intersect at the Storm's Creek inlet of Lake Vesuvius, you can combine an arm of each trail to create a loop hike. Combining the west arm of the **Lakeshore Trail** and the north arm of the **Backpack Trail** (using the **Aldrich Cutoff**) yields a hike of 11 miles. Combining the east arm of the **Lakeshore Trail** and the south arm of the **Back-**pack Trail yields a total hike of 7.5 miles.

Directions:

Lake Vesuvius Recreation Area lies 1 mile east of S.R. 93, 6 miles north of Ironton (or 39 miles south of Jackson). Drive east on the entry road for .9 mile and bear left onto the road that leads toward the Boat Dock and Beach. Proceed .4 mile and park in the Boat Dock parking area, just northwest of the Dam (see map).

165

APPENDIX I
Synopsis of Natural History

The following pages provide a brief overview of Earth's natural history. While emphasis is placed on events in Ohio, a global perspective is necessitated by their relationship to worldwide evolutionary patterns. Indeed, the study of natural history teaches us that the character and quality of our local environment cannot be divorced from the status of ecosystems across the planet. Any effort to protect Ohio's natural resources must not ignore the impact of global factors.

PRECAMBRIAN ERA (4600 to 600 MYA*)

Earth's first 4 billion years were characterized by gradual cooling of the planet's crust, evolution of the atmosphere and formation of the primordial oceans. Life first appeared some 3.6 billion years ago, protected from the sun's ultraviolet radiation by the nourishing seas themselves. Among the earliest forms were cyanobacteria which, through the process of photosynthesis, enriched the atmosphere with oxygen.

PALEOZOIC ERA (600 to 225 MYA)

Ohio's bedrock is composed entirely of sediments from Paleozoic seas. During this Era, shallow oceans bathed the continents and their sediments compacted into the shales, limestones, dolomites and sandstones that we find today. Geologists divide the Paleozoic Era into 7 Periods:

Cambrian Period (600 to 500 MYA). Cambrian rocks underlie all of Ohio but have since been covered by younger sedimentary rocks. Tropical seas of the Cambrian witnessed the rise of small marine invertebrates, especially the trilobites.

Ordovician Period (500 to 400 MYA). An upward "bowing" of the Precambrian rock below southwestern Ohio, known as the "Cincinnati Arch," has kept Ordovician sediments near the surface and the limestones and shales of this Period are exposed for study throughout the Greater Cincinnati area. Bryozoans, trilobites, brachiopods and other primitive marine invertebrates abound in these ancient deposits.

Silurian Period (440 to 400 MYA). Limestones, dolomites and shales dominate the Silurian sedimentary rocks which are exposed throughout much of western Ohio; Clifton Gorge and Paint Creek State Park are excellent places to study them. Increasing atmospheric oxygen led to the formation of the ozone layer which permitted primitive land plants to colonize the coastal areas. The first marine vertebrates appeared during this Period and stranded Silurian seas left behind huge deposits of salt and gypsum across northern Ohio.

Devonian Period (400 to 350 MYA). Known as the "Age of Fishes," Devonian seas harbored the first bony fish, sharks and lung fish. Primitive amphibians, ferns and the first tree-like plants evolved during the Devonian Period. Columbus limestone of the Marblehead peninsula and Erie Islands and Ohio shale of central and northeastern Ohio formed from Devonian sea deposits.

*million years ago

Mississippian Period (350 to 310 MYA). Shallow seas across eastern Ohio deposited shales and sandstones, including the famous Blackhand Sandstone of south-central Ohio and Berea sandstone of the Cuyahoga Valley. Proliferation of land plants set the stage for the first thin coal seams in the bedrock of this Period. Indeed, the Mississippian and Pennsylvanian Periods are often referred to as the **Carboniferous Period.**

Pennsylvanian Period (310 to 270 MYA). Tree-sized ferns, giant horsetails and extensive swamplands covered much of eastern Ohio and would later yield the coal seams of the Appalachian Plateau. Huge amphibians and earth's first insects inhabited the swamps and primitive coniferous woodlands spread across the globe. Pennsylvanian rocks are exposed for study at Salt Fork State Park, Chapin State Forest and the Virginia Kendall Ledges, among other places. Iron oxides in the Pennsylvanian sandstones of southeastern Ohio gave rise to the Iron Belt communities of Hope Furnace and Vesuvius (see Hikes 59 & 64).

Permian Period (270 to 225 MYA). As the Permian Period dawned, Africa was crunching into the eastern edge of North America, folding and uplifting the Southern Appalachians. Only the easternmost counties of Ohio were covered by Permian seas and the limestones, shales and sandstones of that region represent the youngest bedrock in the State. The first small reptiles evolved during the Permian and, by its close, Earth's continents had merged into the mega-continent of Pangea.

MESOZOIC ERA (225 to 65 MYA)

Christened the "Age of Reptiles," the Mesozoic is divided into 3 Periods. Either Ohio remained above sea level throughout the Mesozoic or sediments from this era have long since eroded from the surface.

Triassic Period (225 to 190 MYA). A hot, dry climate favored further evolution and dominance of the reptiles. Primitive crocodiles, turtles and small, herbivorous dinosaurs appeared.

Jurassic Period (190 to 135 MYA). Allosaurus, brontosaurus, stegasaurus, pleisiosaurus and the pterysaurs evolved. Conifers reached their evolutionary peak and flowering plants made their first appearance. Early in the Jurassic, Pangea split into Laurasia (future North America-Europe-Asia) and Gondwana-land (future South America-Africa-Antarctica-Australia). Late in the Period, Africa split from Gondwanaland and drifted northward, joining the Laurasian continents.

The Jurassic also witnessed the emergence of small, shrew-like creatures, the first primitive mammals.

Cretaceous Period (135 to 65 MYA). By the onset of the Cretaceous, North America had assumed its present position. Horned dinosaurs and Tyrannosaurus rex appeared. Primitive monotremes and marsupials evolved in Gondwanaland while early eutherians (placental mammals) spread across Laurasia. India broke from Gondwanaland approximately 80 MYA and drifted toward the north. By the close of the Period, cooling of the Earth's climate ushered in the demise of the dinosaurs and the rise of the mammals.

CENOZOIC ERA (65 MYA to Present)

Known as the "Age of Mammals," the Cenozoic is divided into 7 Epochs; the first five Epochs are grouped within the **Tertiary Period** while the last two comprise the **Quarternary Period.**

Paleocene Epoch (65 to 54 MYA). Ancestral primates appeared in Africa. The Rocky Mountains began to rise and Australia split from Antarctica, drifting into prolonged isolation.

Eocene Epoch (54 to 38 MYA). Primitive elephants evolved in Africa where another mammalian group, the cetaceans (whales, dolphins, seals) were returning to the sea. Rodents, bats and early carnivorous mammals first appeared in the Eocene. By the close of the Epoch, ice was forming on Antarctica.

Oligocene Epoch (38 to 22 MYA). Continued cooling of the climate and periods of glaciation characterized the Epoch. Grass evolved in the "rain shadow" of the Rocky Mountains and primitive horses, rhinocerous and camels emerged from the forests of North America to feast on the boundless prairies. In doing so, they evolved into larger species, better adapted to life in the open country.

Miocene Epoch (22 to 10 MYA). The first true monkeys evolved in Africa and India slammed into southern Asia, forcing up the Himalayas. Late in the Epoch, further cooling of the earth's climate led to extensive ice formation across Antarctica and a subsequent lowering of the sea level. The Bering land bridge opened and an interchange of Asian and North American species occurred.

Pliocene Epoch (10 to 2 MYA). Ice was now forming at the North Pole for the first time and continued lowering of the sea uncovered the Isthmus of Panama. Sloths, armadillos and opossums spread northward while mastodons, tapirs and llamas headed south. As the Sierra Nevada was pushing skyward in western North America, the first hominids (upright walking apes) appeared in Africa.

Pleistocene Epoch (2 to .01 MYA). Often called the "Ice Age," glaciers advanced into Ohio four times during the Pleistocene. The Nebraskan ice sheet nipped northern Ohio approximately 2 million years ago. The Kansan glacier plowed deep into western Ohio approximately 1.2 MYA, blocking the course of the Teays River. This massive River headed in the Appalachian highlands of Virginia and flowed northwestward through Ohio, entering near Portsmouth and exiting west of Grand Lake St. Marys. Blocked by ice, the waters of the Teays network diverted to the south, creating the Ohio River System.

The Illinoian (400,000 years ago) and Wisconsin (70,000 years ago) glaciers pushed into northern and western Ohio, scouring the landscape, diverting streams, carving new valleys and enriching the soil with their till. As the Wisconsin ice sheet retreated into Canada, some 12-15,000 years ago, it left glacial lakes, meltwater gorges, moraines of till and erratic boulders in its wake (see Hikes at Kelleys Island, Clifton Gorge, and Stages Pond).

In addition to altering the landscape, the glaciers "consumed" a great deal of water, causing sea levels to fall some 400 feet below current depths. This opened land bridges between the continents, permitting the gradual migration, interaction and exchange of species. Among the mammals that crossed from Asia to North America were the first human Americans. Man evolved in east Africa during the latter half of the Pleistocene; by the end of the Epoch his influence was felt across Europe, Asia and the Americas.

Holocene Epoch (10,000 years ago to Present). The first Americans were likely south of the Wisconsin glacier by 15-20,000 years ago. Among these original pioneers were the Paleo-hunters, descendents of the Asthapascans, who hunted mammoths and bison across the vast Plains. By the onset of the Holocene, native Americans had adopted an "Archaic" lifestyle, with relatively permanent settlements. Early Ohioans included the Hopewell and Adenan cultures, known collectively as the "mound-builders," whose ceremonial and burial earthworks can still be seen today (see Ft. Ancient, Shawnee Lookout and Fort Hill hikes). Modern Indian tribes did not settle in Ohio until the close of the 17th Century. Shawnee Indians occupied southern Ohio, arriving from the mid-Atlantic region. The Miami tribe moved into western Ohio from the upper Mississippi Valley and the Wyandots spread southward from Canada, settling in north-central and north-western Ohio. Finally, the Delaware Indians, arriving from the east, occupied the Muskingum Valley.

Just over 200 years ago, the most destructive creature in the life of our planet, "civilized man," charged across the Appalachians to conquer the West with his gun, axe and plow. The rest is history.

APPENDIX II

OHIO CONSERVATION ORGANIZATIONS

This is a **partial list** of organizations that are dedicated to the protection and preservation of Ohio's natural resources. The list is restricted to those groups that are mentioned in this guide. Many others are active across the State and are equally deserving of your time and financial support.

The Audubon Society, Aullwood Audubon Center & Farm, 1000 Aullwood Road, Dayton, Ohio 45411; 513-890-7360

Buckeye Trail Association, P.O. Box 254, Worthington, Ohio 43085

Cincinnati Museum of Natural History, 1301 Western Ave., Cincinnati, Ohio 45203

Cincinnati Nature Center, 4949 Tealtown Road, Milford, Ohio 45150; 513-831-1711

Cleveland Metroparks System, 4101 Fulton Parkway, Cleveland, Ohio 44144-1923; 216-351-6300

Cleveland Museum of Natural History, Wade Oval, University Circle, Cleveland, Ohio 44106; 216-231-4600

Cuyahoga Valley National Recreation Area, 15610 Vaughn Road, Brecksville, Ohio 44141-3018

Dayton-Montgomery County Park District, 1375 East Siebenthaler Avenue, Dayton, Ohio 45414; 513-278-8231

Dysart Woods Laboratory, Department of Botany, Porter Hall, Ohio University, Athens, Ohio 45701; 614-594-5821

Geauga Park District, 9420 Robinson Road, Chardon, Ohio 44024; 216-286-9504

Hamilton County Park District, 10245 Winton Road, Cincinnati, Ohio 45231; 513-563-4513 (East); 513-385-4811 (West)

Holden Arboretum, 9500 Sperry Road, Mentor, Ohio 44060; 216-946-4400

Little Miami, Inc., 3012 Section Road, at French Park, Cincinnati, Ohio 45237; 513-351-6400

Metroparks of Columbus & Franklin County, P.O. Box 29169, Columbus, Ohio 43229; 614-891-0700

Metropark District of the Toledo Area, 5100 W. Central Ave., Toledo, Ohio 43615; 419-535-3050

Metroparks Serving Summit County, 975 Treaty Line Road, Akron, Ohio 44313; 216-867-5511

Miami County Park District, 2535 E. Ross Road, Tipp City, Ohio 45371; 513-667-1086

Miami Purchase Association, Hamilton County Memorial Building, 1225 Elm St., Cincinnati, Ohio 45210; 513-721-4506

The Nature Conservancy, Ohio Chapter, 1504 W. First Ave., Columbus, Ohio 43212; 614-486-4194

Ohio Department of Natural Resources, Division of Natural Areas and Preserves, Fountain Square, Building F, Columbus, Ohio 43224; 614-265-6453

Ohio Department of Natural Resources, Division of Parks & Recreation, Fountain Square, Columbus, Ohio 43224; 614-256-7000

Ohio Department of Natural Resources, Division of Wildlife, Fountain Square, Building C-4, Columbus, Ohio 43224

Ohio Historical Society, 1982 Velma Ave., Columbus, Ohio 43211; 614-297-2300

Ottawa National Wildlife Refuge, 14000 West State Route 2, Oak Harbor, Ohio 43449; 419-898-0014

Oxbow, Inc., P.O. Box 43391, Cincinnati, Ohio 45243; 513-471-8001

Rails-to-Trails Conservancy, Ohio Chapter, Suite 307, 36 West Gay St., Columbus, Ohio 43215; 614-224-8707

Rivers Unlimited, 3012 Section Road, at French Park, Cincinnati, Ohio 45237; 513-351-4417

Wayne National Forest, Ironton District, 710 Park Ave., Ironton, Ohio 45638; 614-532-3223

The Wilderness Center, 9877 Alabama Ave., SW, P.O. Box 202, Wilmot, Ohio 44689-0202; 216-359-5235

BIBLIOGRAPHY

1. Attenborough, David, **Life on Earth**, Little, Brown & Co., 1979

2. Brennan, Louis A., **American Dawn, A New Model of American Prehistory**, Macmillan, N.Y., 1970

3. Buckeye Trail Association, Inc., **More Short Hikes on the Buckeye Trail**, Worthington, Ohio, 1978

4. Carman, J. Ernest, **The Geologic Interpretation of Scenic Features in Ohio**, Ohio Department of Natural Resources, Reprint Series #3, 1972

5. Corbett, Robert G. and Barbara M. Manner, **Geology and Habitats of the Cuyahoga Valley National Recreation Area, Ohio**, Ohio J. Science, 88 (1): 40-47, 1988

6. Dineley, David, **Earth's Voyage Through Time**, Alfred A. Knopf, Inc., 1973

7. Farb, Peter, **Face of North America, The Natural History of a Continent**, Harper & Row, 1963

8. Folzenlogen, Darcy & Robert, **Walking Cincinnati, 52 Scenic Hikes Through Our Parks & Neighborhoods**, Willow Press, 1989

9. Gleason, H.A. and A. Cronquist, **The Natural Geography of Plants**, Columbia University Press, 1964

10. Hannibal, Joseph T. and Rodney M. Feldmann, **The Cuyahoga Valley National Recreation Area, Ohio: Devonian and Carboniferous clastic rocks**, Geological Society of America Centennial Field Guide, North-Central Section, 1987

11. Jones, J. Knox and Elmer C. Birney, **Handbook of Mammals of the North-Central States**, University of Minnesota Press, Minneapolis, 1988

12. Kricher, J.C. and G. Morrison, **Eastern Forests**, Peterson Field Guides, Houghton Mifflin Company, Boston, 1988

13. Larocque, A. and M. Fisher Marple, **Ohio Fossils**, Ohio Department of Natural Resources, Division of Geologic Survey, Columbus, 1955; 10th Printing, 1977

14. Madson, John, **Where the Sky Began, Land of the Tallgrass Prairie**, Sierra Club Books, 1982

15. McPhee, John, **In Suspect Terrain**, McGraw-Hill, Ryerson LTD, Toronto; Farrar Straus Giroux, New York, 1982, 1983, 1986

16. Melvin, Ruth W., **A Guide to Ohio Outdoor Education Areas**, 2nd Edition, Ohio Department of Natural Resources and the Ohio Academy of Science

17. Rails-to-Trails Conservancy, **A Map and Guide to Ohio's Rails-Trails**, 1989

18. Ruchhoft, R.H., **Backpack Loops in Southern Ohio**, Pucelle Press, 1984

19. Shimer, John A., **Field Guide to Landforms in the United States**, The Macmillan Company, New York, 1972

20. Stearn, C.S., R.L. Carrol and T.H. Clark, **Geological Evolution of North America**, 3rd Edition, John Wiley & Sons, Inc., 1979

21. Walton, Debra et al., **A Guide to the Ohio Preserves of the Nature Conservancy**, Ohio Chapter, The Nature Conservancy, Columbus, Ohio

22. Weller, Milton W., **Freshwater Marshes, Ecology & Wildlife Management**, University of Minnesota Press, 1981

Index

The following is a "Functional Index." Rather than relisting all the preserves, trails, streams, etc. that are mentioned in this guide, this Index lists geologic, topographic, vegetative and cultural features that are highlighted throughout the book. Each is followed by the numbered Hiking Areas in which they appear.